HISTORY NOTES

Richard Wilcox

A STUDY GUIDE TO ACCOMPANY

THE
WESTERN HERITAGE

VOLUME ONE: TO 1740

TEACHING AND LEARNING CLASSROOM EDITION
BRIEF FOURTH EDITION

Donald Kagan

Steven Ozment

Frank M. Turner

PEARSON

Prentice Hall

Upper Saddle River, New Jersey 07458

© 2005 by PEARSON EDUCATION, INC.
Upper Saddle River, New Jersey 07458

ISBN 0-13-132198-6

Printed in the United States of America

CONTENTS

Chapter 1
THE BIRTH OF CIVILIZATION

Practice Test

1. The earliest period in cultural development was the
    (a) Neolithic Age.
    (b) Paleolithic Age.
    (c) Bronze Age.
    (d) Mesopotamian Age.

2. Division of labor between the sexes appears to have initiated through the manner of
    (a) obtaining different foodstuffs.
    (b) making tools and weapons.
    (c) making clothing.
    (d) child-bearing.

3. The so-called Neolithic Revolution clearly produced
    (a) increased disease.
    (b) a decline in world population.
    (c) a dramatic increase in world population.
    (d) the preconditions for the emergence of civilization.

4. The beginning of civilization includes all of the following EXCEPT
    (a) urbanism.
    (b) the writing system.
    (c) democracy.
    (d) long-distance trade.

5. The earliest Mesopotamian kingdoms were commonly ruled by
    (a) popular generals.
    (b) priest-kings.
    (c) local assemblies.
    (d) scribes.

6. The pyramids of Egypt are an invaluable source of information about that civilization for they indicate
    (a) great technical skill.
    (b) the extent of royal power.
    (c) the enormous wealth of the pharaoh.
    (d) all of the above

7. Hieroglyphics, the sacred writing of ancient Egypt
    (a)   were only carved inside the pyramids.
    (b)   were designed to record the bounty of harvests and trade.
    (c)   was difficult to master because its symbols stood for many different things.
    (d)   were purely mathematical in scope.

8. The peoples of the ancient Near East, especially noted for their cruelty and brutality were the
    (a)   Mitannians.
    (b)   Assyrians.
    (c)   Hittites.
    (d)   Phoenicians.

9. The end of the Babylonian Captivity of the Jews occurred when
    (a)   the Jews were released from bondage in Babylon by the Persians.
    (b)   Moses led his people out of Egypt.
    (c)   the state of Israel was formed in 1948.
    (d)   Jews abandoned their belief in a Messiah.

10. Ancient literature appears to suggest that the function of mankind is to
    (a)   understand the gods.
    (b)   develop their own lives.
    (c)   control nature.
    (d)   serve the gods.

True/False

_____1.   Water was Mesopotamia's lifeline.

_____2.   The Mesopotamians based their mathematical system on a sexagesimal system.

_____3.   Mesopotamian slaves were mainly captives of war.

_____4.   Mesopotamians believed they would be rewarded for good deeds in the afterlife.

_____5.   Throughout Egyptian history the god Aten was of singular importance.

_____6.   Pharaohs were exclusively females in Egypt.

_____7.   During the period of the New Kingdom, pharaohs continued to erect pyramids that emphasized their graves.

_____8.   The Hebrew prophetic tradition asserted that God would redeem His people and would restore the House of David through the coming of Jesus Christ.

_____ 9. The Jews believed that their God was a merciful God and judged people according to how they treated others.

_____ 10. Hippocrates believed that all diseases could be found to have a supernatural cause.

Completion

1. The _____ Revolution can be thought of as the Age of Agriculture.

2. The first civilization founded in Mesopotamia was that of the _____ .

3. The first ruling dynasty of Sumer and Akkad developed from the king _____.

4. _____ is considered history's first identifiable author.

5. The Eighteenth Dynasty of Egypt saw an interesting religious revolt led by the pharaoh _____ .

6. The modern religions of Judaism, Christianity, and Islam have their origins in the area of _____ .

7. _____ were an important trading people who had developed a simplified writing system.

8. The greatest contribution of the Jews in the area of religious ideas is _____ .

9. According to one Egyptian legend, the god Re, though relenting, once attempted to destroy humanity through the goddess _____ .

10. _____ was the first Greek philosopher.

When?

1. The earliest period in cultural development—the Paleolithic Age—began with the first use of stone tools about a millions years ago and lasted until about
    (a) 10000 BCE.
    (b) 5000 BCE.
    (c) 11000 BCE.
    (d) 1000 BCE.

2. The Middle Kingdom in Egypt lasted from
    (a) 2200-2025 BCE.
    (b) 2700-2200 BCE.
    (c) 2025-1630 BCE.
    (d) 1550-1075 BCE.

3. The Bronze Age lasted from
    (a) 3000-1000 BCE.
    (b) 3100-1200 BCE.
    (c) 3100-1100 BCE.
    (d) 3000-1200 BCE.

4. In what year did Israel's 10 lost tribes disappear?
    (a) 720 BCE
    (b) 721 BCE
    (c) 722 BCE
    (d) 723 BCE

5. Writing first appeared in Egypt about
    (a) 4000 BCE.
    (b) 3000 BCE.
    (c) 2000 BCE.
    (d) 1000 BCE.

Matching

Match the term to its definition.

1. Paleolithic	a) new stone age
2. Bronze Age	b) increasing importance on metal
3. Cuneiform	c) old stone
4. Pharaoh	d) very first writing system
5. Neolithic	e) god-king of ancient Egypt

Map Labeling (map 1-1)

Using the map below (and your textbook) answer the following questions.

1. It is believed that civilization first appeared here.

2. What was considered the earliest urban center?

3. The first monarchs were in which city?

4. The final flowering of Sumerian civilization was in which city?

5. Where would you find the new Amorite dynasties?

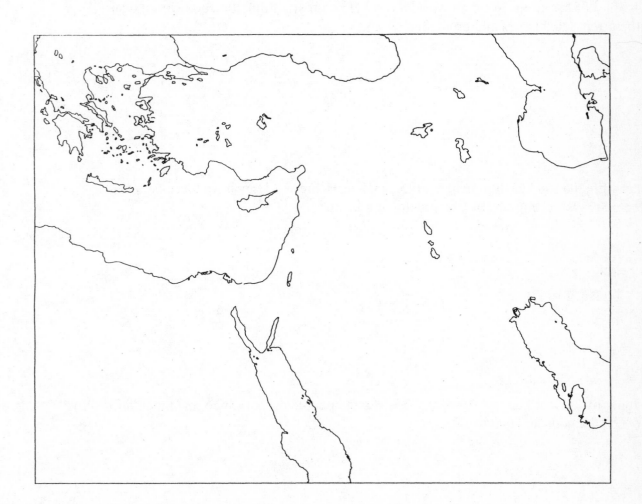

How and Why

1. Describe the movement of early Neolithic peoples to the river-watered lowlands. What caused this movement? What factors were operating that brought about the rise of cities in these river valleys?

2. From your perspective, how does the law code of Hammurabi relate to established principles of law in the Western world today? How do you think the code would deal with current legal issues and problems?

3. What were the fundamental beliefs of the ancient Hebrews? How have these beliefs affected the later religions of Christianity and Islam?

4. Judging by ancient literary examples, how did the people of that time view the relationship between the gods and themselves?

5. How does the Greek outlook on the relationship of humankind to nature differ from that of other ancient Near Eastern peoples?

Chapter 2
THE RISE OF GREEK CIVILIZATION

Practice Test

1. One of the basic differences between Minoan and Mycenaean civilizations is that the latter peoples were
   - (a) more interested in beauty and truth.
   - (b) more dependent on trade.
   - (c) more warlike.
   - (d) actually they were similar in most ways.

2. The entire character of the late Helladic period was changed by the so-called invasion of the
   - (a) Cretans.
   - (b) Persians.
   - (c) Dorians.
   - (d) Macedonians.

3. The worst class to belong to in Homeric society was
   - (a) slaves.
   - (b) thetes.
   - (c) landless agricultural laborers.
   - (d) all of the above.

4. Homer's value system incorporated all of the following EXCEPT
   - (a) courage.
   - (b) defense of honor.
   - (c) physical prowess.
   - (d) modesty.

5. As the high point of Greek civilization approached, the center of political and social life was the
   - (a) agora.
   - (b) acropolis.
   - (c) symposion.
   - (d) palaestra.

6. An important continuous factor in the political life of Athens appears to have been the rivalry between
   - (a) tyrants.
   - (b) generals.
   - (c) great Athenian families.
   - (d) priests.

7. _____ founded the great Persian Empire in the mid-sixth century BCE
    (a) Cyrus
    (b) Xerxes
    (c) Croesus
    (d) Darius

8. The origin of the Persian Wars is generally attributed to
    (a) internal political problems in Athens.
    (b) Greek support for the Ionian rebellion.
    (c) Persia's attempt to take advantage of the rivalry between Athens and Sparta.
    (d) internal political problems in Persia.

9. Which is the correct chronological sequence of these major battles of the Persian Wars?
    (a) Plataea, Salamis, Thermopylae, Marathon
    (b) Salamis, Plataea, Marathon, Thermopylae
    (c) Marathon, Thermopylae, Salamis, Plataea
    (d) Thermopylae, Mycale, Salamis, Marathon

10. Let us assume a Persian victory against the Greek city-states. Which of the following most accurately depicts what, in your opinion, would have happened?
    (a) It would have little effect since the major Greek contributions to the West had already been made before the fifth century BCE
    (b) It probably would have reduced the Greeks to near servitude, but would have stimulated cultural growth.
    (c) It would have stimulated Greek cultural freedom and development in any event.
    (d) none of the above

True-False

_____ 1. The Minoans were Greek.

_____ 2. "You with a dog's face and a deer's heart," is part of Achilles' address to the commander of the expedition against Troy.

_____ 3. Homeric kings exercised great power over their Greek subjects.

_____ 4. A short spear was the normal weapon of a hoplite.

_____ 5. Spartan boys normally began their military training at the age of seven.

_____ 6. The Greeks of the Dark Ages explored the idea of popular government.

_____ 7. Homer wrote *Works and Days*.

_____ 8. Kings governed Sparta.

_____9. Miltiades was the Athenian commander at Marathon.

_____10. During the Persian Wars, the Athenian Themistocies urged his city-state to imitate Sparta and rely on the army.

Completion

1. The most striking feature of Cretan civilization is evidenced by their _____.

2. The world of the Mycenaeans is better understood today because of the discovery at Cnossus of tablets known as _____.

3. "Always be the best and distinguished above others," can be associated with the tales of _____.

4. The most important military advance during this early period of Greek history was in the _____.

5. The Greek _____ were responsible for the transfer of power from the aristocracy to the broader elements of the polis.

6. A sixth-century BCE Greek seeking advice about the future would probably travel to _____.

7. _____ was the Greek god of excessive pleasures.

8. Theognis of Megara actually divided everyone into two classes of people, the _____ and the _____.

9. In the battle of Thermopylae Pass, the city-state of _____ sacrificed a king and 300 soldiers.

10. The fate of Greece was decided in a sea battle which took place in the straits between _____ and the island of _____.

Matching

Match the god/goddess to his or her correct title.

Zeus	God of Strife
Demeter	Cunning Messenger God
Hera	Goddess of Agriculture and Marriage
Ares	A Sky God
Hermes	Zeus's wife and sister

When

1. The so-call Greek "dark ages" occurred in the period
    (a) 1500-1100 BCE
    (b) 1100-750 BCE
    (c) 750-500 BCE
    (d) 500-250 BCE

2. It is believed that Homer lived in this century BCE.
    (a) eleventh.
    (b) tenth.
    (c) ninth.
    (d) eighth.

3. The Mycenaeans reached their height of power between
    (a) 1400 and 1100 BCE.
    (b) 1300 and 1200 BCE.
    (c) 1400 and 1200 BCE.
    (d) 1500 and 1400 BCE.

4. It is believed that poleis first appeared early in the
    (a) seventh century BCE.
    (b) eighth century BCE.
    (c) ninth century BCE.
    (d) tenth century BCE.

5. By which year BCE did the Persian threat to Greece appeared to have passed?
    (a) 480
    (b) 479
    (c) 478
    (d) 477

Map Labeling (map 2-2)

Using the map below, answer the following by labeling the map.

1. Label the two major cities that were vitally important to Greek civilization

2. Label the area on the map that was called Magna Graecia—Great Greece.

3. Which island was leveled by Darius?

4. Which group of Greeks lived on the western coast of Asia Minor? Add them to the map.

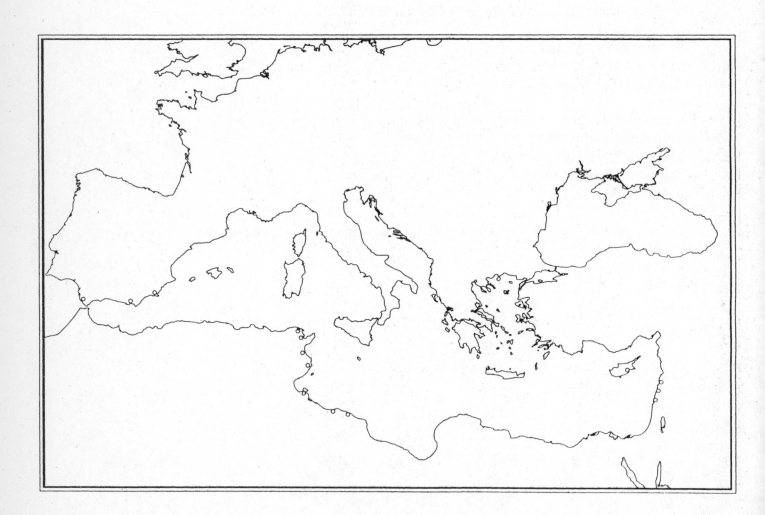

How and Why

1. Modern scholars have suggested several theories to explain the apparent destruction of Mycenaean civilization. Describe and discuss several of these theories.

2. Discuss the idea of the "hero" in Greek literature and thought.

3. What was the Greek view of the concept of citizenship? How is this concept similar to and how is it different from that of the Egyptians and Mesopotamians, and from today's concept?

4. How did the battle of Marathon affect the Athenians? How did it affect the Persians? From a military point of view, how were the Greek city-states with all of their rivalies able to defeat the great empire of Persia?

5. Compare and contrast the world of early Greek civilization (1500–500 BCE) with the early development of the civilizations in Mesopotamia and Egypt.

Chapter 3
CLASSICAL AND HELLENISTIC GREECE

Practice Test

1. With the end of the Persian threat, the Greek world divided into spheres of influence dominated by
    (a) Thebes and Thrace.
    (b) Athens and Sparta.
    (c) Sparta and Corinth.
    (d) Athens and Macedonia.

2. The almost continuous success of Pericles as an elected leader of Athens can be attributed primarily to his
    (a) willingness to use corruption for his own advancement.
    (b) subtle use of police power against all opposition.
    (c) skill as a general and politician
    (d) open contempt toward philosophers.

3. What common theme ran throughout art, literature, and the lives of the Greeks during the Classical Period?
    (a) calm
    (b) serenity
    (c) tension
    (d) all of the above

4. The increased Macedonian wealth of the fourth century BCE derived from
    (a) piracy.
    (b) internal taxation.
    (c) gold and silver mines.
    (d) corrupt politicians.

5. The League of Corinth's constitution promised
    (a) freedom from tribute and military occupation.
    (b) aid in suppressing piracy.
    (c) autonomy in local affairs.
    (d) all of the above

6. Hellenistic culture tended to be
    (a) mainly a rural one.
    (b) concentrated in Greece proper.
    (c) limited to the Athenian state.
    (d) rooted in the cities of Alexander's empire.

7. In the philosophy of Stoicism, the principal aim of man is
   (a) a virtuous life.
   (b) a pleasurable life.
   (c) a life of religious devotion.
   (d) none of the above

8. Hellenistic kings relied on the grid plan to found cities and rebuild old ones. The person responsible for this plan was
   (a) Heraclides.
   (b) Zeno of Citium.
   (c) Epicurus.
   (d) Hippodamus of Miletus.

9. In the Middle Ages, travelers could depend on accurate maps by
   (a) Heraclides of Pontus.
   (b) Hipparchus of Nicaea.
   (c) Erathosthenes of Cyrene.
   (d) none of the above

10. A clearly recognizable sun-centered (heliocentric) view of the universe is associated with
    (a) Aristotle.
    (b) Ptolemy of Alexandria.
    (c) Euclid.
    (d) Aristarchus of Samos.

True/False

_____1. Though Athens gained a strategic advantage, the alliance with Megara brought on the First Peloponnesian War.

_____2. The popular courts of Athens to which any citizen could appeal contained between 51 and 1501 jurors.

_____3. While Athenian women had no choice of husbands, they retained control of their dowry throughout the marriage.

_____4. For Empedocles of Acragas the four basic elements were: fire, earth, love, and strife.

_____5. The leading playwright of the so-called New Comedy of the late fourth century BCE was Menander.

_____6. When compared to Socrates and Plato, Aristotle actually had the longest lifespan.

_____7. Aristotle founded the "Academy."

_____8. The longer pike of thirteen feet utilized by the Macedonians was called a choregos.

_____9. Neither skepticism nor cynicism had much appeal to the city dweller of the third-century BCE.

_____10. Hellenistic contributions to our knowledge of geography can be said to originate in the works of Euclid.

Completion

1. _____ , son of Mitiades, became the leading Athenian soldier and statesman soon after the war with Persia.

2. _____ dominated the Greek mainland and _____ ruled the Aegean Sea in about 446 BCE.

3. _____ was considered the first philosopher.

4. _____ wrote the history of the Great Peloponnesian War.

5. The humility and disdain for worldly things exemplified by Socrates was carried to extremes by _____ and the _____ .

6. One of the reasons for the success of the Macedonian army was an innovative change in the traditional Greek _____ .

7. _____ of Athens believed that a Greek-supported Macedonian invasion of Persia would yield beneficial economic and political results.

8. The _____ believed that nothing could be truly known.

9. Epicurean philosophy attempted to eliminate one's fear of _____ .

10. For the Stoics, the guiding principle in nature was divine reason, or _____ .

When

1. Athens made peace with Persia in
   (a)   446 BCE.
   (b)   445 BCE.
   (c)   449 BCE.
   (d)   450 BCE.

2. The Sophists, a group of teachers, flourished during the
    (a)   early fifth century BCE.
    (b)   mid-fifth century BCE.
    (c)   late fifth century BCE.
    (d)   early fourth century BCE.

3. The Great Peloponnesian War lasted from
    (a)   460-445 BCE.
    (b)   432-404 BCE.
    (c)   404-403 BCE.
    (d)   336-323 BCE.

4. Alexander the Great's reign lasted
    (a)   10 years.
    (b)   11 years.
    (c)   12 years.
    (d)   13 years.

5. The First Peloponnesian War lasted from
    (a)   460-445 BCE.
    (b)   432-404 BCE.
    (c)   404-403 BCE.
    (d)   336-323 BCE.

Matching

Match the philosopher to his belief system.

Thales	the world is composed of permanent elements
Heraclitus	the world is constantly evolving from potentiality to actuality
Sophists	permanence is an illusion
Socrates	all things come from a single universal substance: water
Empedocles	truth and the power of reason
Aristotle	the art of persuasion through rhetoric

Map Labeling

Using Map 3-1, label the following:

Three areas that were independent members of the Athenian Empire

Three areas that were dependent members of the Athenian Empire

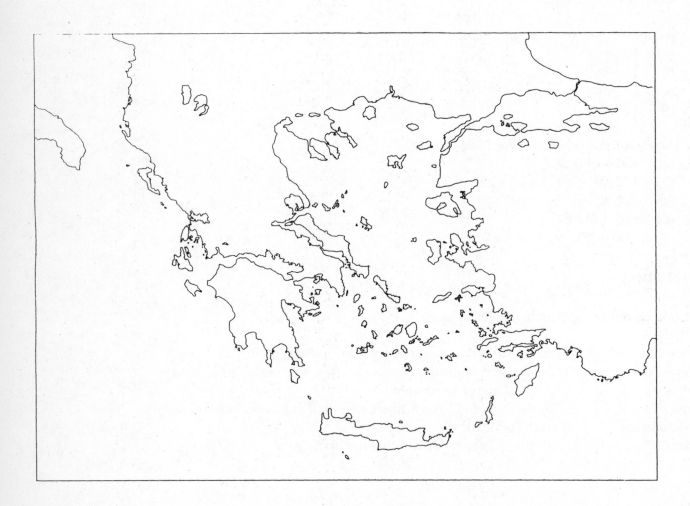

How and Why

1. Discuss in detail the causes and overall effects of the Peloponnesian Wars.

2. Herodotus and Thucydides are considered founders of the modern concept of history. What difficulties would they have encountered in preparing their histories as compared to modern scholars and students today?

3. From your understanding of the activities and achievements of Alexander of Macedon, does he deserve the title of "great"? Explain your answer fully.

4. How does Hellenistic philosophy as expressed through the teachings of the Stoics and Epicureans differ from that of classical Greece?

5. Describe the overall characteristics of the Hellenistic world's lifestyle and outlook. What were the main contributions to the West of the Hellenistic age?

Chapter 4
ROME: FROM REPUBLIC TO EMPIRE

Practice Test

1. Which group of Romans could serve as priests, senators, and magistrates?
    (a) plebeians
    (b) clientage
    (c) patricians
    (d) women

2. Ultimately, the Roman Republic came to be dominated by
    (a) the consuls.
    (b) the senatorial aristocracy.
    (c) the army.
    (d) the tribunes of the people.

3. The worst military defeat in Roman history occurred during the wars with Carthage at
    (a) the Ebro River.
    (b) the Ticinus River.
    (c) Zama.
    (d) Cannae.

4. The Roman general Publius Cornelius Scipio (Africanus) was successful in the Second Punic War because
    (a) he was a talented military leader.
    (b) he captured New Carthage in Spain.
    (c) he was able to win support from former enemies.
    (d) all of the above

5. Roman education was designed to make young boys
    (a) patriotic and law-abiding.
    (b) moral and pious.
    (c) respectful of Roman tradition.
    (d) all of the above

6. Near the end of the Roman Republic slaves accounted for _____ of the population of Italy.
    (a) 20 percent
    (b) 30 percent
    (c) 40 percent
    (d) 50 percent

7. Central to the reform program of the Gracchi brothers was
    (a) redistribution of land.
    (b) freeing of slaves.
    (c) increased authority for tribunes.
    (d) reduction of senatorial power.

8. The fall of the Roman Republic was due in part to the rivalries of
    (a) ambitious generals.
    (b) demagogic tribunes.
    (c) influential equestrians.
    (d) all of the above

9. Of approximately 900 senators, about _____ were involved in the plot to murder Julius Caesar.
    (a) 6
    (b) 36
    (c) 60
    (d) 600

10. The Second Triumvirate was composed of
    (a) Pompey, Brutus, Cassius.
    (b) Octavian, Brutus, Lepidus.
    (c) Mark Antony, Agrippa, Maecenas.
    (d) Mark Antony, Octavian, Lepidus.

True-False

_____1. Etruscan culture had little effect on Rome.

_____2. Originally, Carthage in North Africa was a Phoenician colony.

_____3. Mercenary soldiers, who considered themselves sons of the war god Mars, were called Martians.

_____4. As the Romans increased their role in the Mediterranean world, it became clear to them that military campaigns could be profitable.

_____5. The murder of Tiberius Gracchus and his followers is an important watershed of the Republic because it was the first politically motivated bloodshed within the state.

_____6. Many volunteers for the Roman legions viewed enlistment as an opportunity to obtain land and other rewards in exchange for their service.

_____7. The initial claim of M. L. Crassus to prominence in Rome stemmed from his defeat of Mithridates.

_____8. The First Triumvirate was formed by Caesar, Pompey, and Mark Antony.

_____9. Caesar's military triumphs in Gaul were possible not only because of his own abilities, but also because of the experience of his officers and men.

_____10. Among his many internal reforms, Caesar substantially increased the number of Roman senators.

Completion

1. The center of Roman life was the _____.

2. Winning a battle, but suffering heavy casualties, is referred to as a _____.

3. Carthage's most talented general was _____.

4. A Greek slave accompanying a young Roman boy to school was called a _____.

5. After the Second Punic, or Carthagenian, War much of Rome's farmland was reorganized into large estates called _____.

6. Success in the Jugurthine War in Numidia helped the political career of _____.

7. _____ led an army of fugitive slaves that defeated several legions and overran most of Italy before it was quelled.

8. In large measure, connections through marriage and in-laws helped the initial political career of _____.

9. The deaths of Antony and Cleopatra left _____ in charge of the Mediterranean world.

10. _____ and _____ are among the better known names of Caesar's murderers.

When

1. Rome evolved during which century?
   (a) early eighth century BCE
   (b) mid-eighth century BCE
   (c) late eighth century BCE
   (d) mid-seventh century BCE

2. In what century were censors given the right to expel inappropriately behaved senators?
   (a)   second BCE
   (b)   third BCE
   (c)   fourth BCE
   (d)   fifth BCE

3. Hasdrubal Bara, Carthaginian governor of Spain, was assassinated in what year?
   (a)   218 BCE
   (b)   219 BCE
   (c)   220 BCE
   (d)   221 BCE

4. During which century did slavery start to decline in Rome?
   (a)   fifth
   (b)   fourth
   (c)   third
   (d)   second

5. The First Triumvirate was founded in
   (a)   60 BCE.
   (b)   59 BCE.
   (c)   58 BCE.
   (d)   57 BCE.

Matching

Match the leader to the battle he won.

Publius Cornelius Scipio	Actium
C. Marins	Battle of Zama
Pompey	Gaul
Caesar	Jugurthine War
Octavio	Slave rebellion led by Spartacus

Map Labeling

Using Map 4-3, answer the following questions by labeling the map.

Label the first 3 provinces of the Roman Empire.

Label the city that Hamilcar Bara restored.

When the Romans violated the Ebro Treaty, they allied themselves with what town? Label it on the map.

Label the port in which the Romans met with disaster.

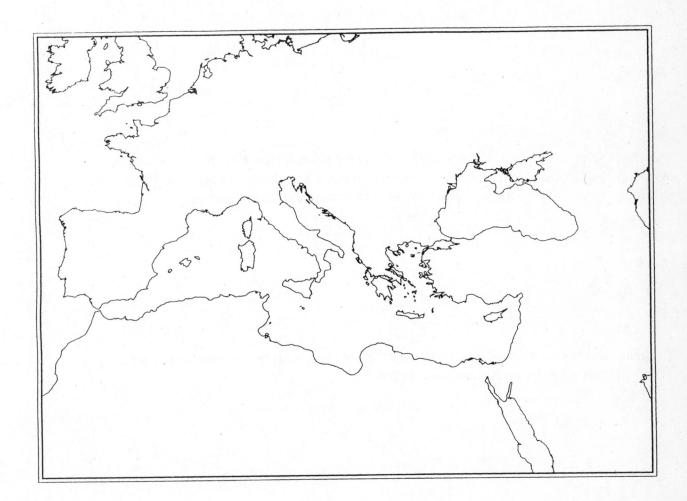

How and Why

1. Describe the Roman Republic's policies toward conquered peoples. Imagine yourself as a Roman senator of this era. What suggestions would you make or endorse with regard to conquered enemies?

2. What were the causes and historical significance of Rome's wars against Carthage?

3. Describe the style of education available in the early Roman Republic. In your opinion, why was the emphasis on young men? Briefly comment on what you see as the key differences between the Roman education of young men and young women?

4. Compare and contrast the origins of the First Triumvirate with the Second Triumvirate. How did each relate to the Roman constitution?

5. In your opinion, was Julius Caesar's threat to the Senate and the political foundations of the Roman Republic real or imagined? Explain your answer fully.

Chapter 5
THE ROMAN EMPIRE

Practice Test

1. The many important changes in the government of Rome during the Augustan Principate had the overall effect of
       (a)   reducing inefficiency.
       (b)   eliminating dangers to peace and order.
       (c)   lessening the distinction between Romans and Italians.
       (d)   all of the above

2. The Roman poet Catullus did NOT
       (a)   celebrate the importance of the individual.
       (b)   write witty exchanges with his acquaintances.
       (c)   show interest in moral instruction.
       (d)   insult contemporaries such as Julius Caesar.

3. Cicerco believed in respecting all of the following except:
       (a)   law.
       (b)   custom.
       (c)   tradition.
       (d)   populares.

4. Jesus of Nazareth taught all of the following EXCEPT
       (a)   the good will be rewarded with immortality.
       (b)   Jews would triumph over their earthly enemies.
       (c)   the faithful must give up their worldliness.
       (d)   practice love, charity, and humility.

5. The original function of the Christian bishop was designed to
       (a)   oversee the Board of Elders.
       (b)   serve as deacon.
       (c)   protect Christians from outside enemies.
       (d)   lead in worship and supervise funds.

6. The men of the Germanic tribes that for a long time lived on the fringes of the Roman
   Empire spent much of their time engaged in
       (a)   farming.
       (b)   pastoral activities.
       (c)   fighting and drinking.
       (d)   none of the above

7. The economy of Rome during these centuries appears to have suffered as a result of
    (a) imposition of new taxes.
    (b) no system of credit.
    (c) little reserve funds beyond normal budget allocations.
    (d) all of the above

8. Which of the following groups of Roman emperors is in correct chronological sequence?
    (a) Theodosius, Decius, Commodus
    (b) Constantine, Diocletian, Theodosius
    (c) Valerian, Diocletian, Julian "The Apostate"
    (d) Commodus, Constantine, Alexander Severus

9. The Christian writer Jerome is best known for his
    (a) peculiar martyrdom.
    (b) Latin version of the Bible.
    (c) religious inspired poetry.
    (d) toleration of pagan ideas.

10. Augustine's The City of God was
    (a) a study of urban society in antiquity.
    (b) a response to pagan charges against Christianity.
    (c) a forecast of the end of the world.
    (d) an explanation of his conversion to Christianity.

True-False

_____1. Under the emperor Augustus, the frontier army of Rome was maintained at just under one million men.

_____2. Because of its theme, Ovid's most popular work was the Ars Amatoria.

_____3. Nero, despite his other shortcomings, was the first Roman emperor to take the offensive against the barbarians.

_____4. Fully one-third of the city of Rome's living space was taken up by the elegant homes of the wealthy.

_____5. One of the great problems facing the early Christians was their relationship with the Jews.

_____6. Roman authorities began the practice of attacking Christians.

_____7. In 260, a newly formed Persian-Iranian dynasty humiliated the Romans with the capture of the emperor Valerian.

_____ 8. With the accession of the emperor Septimius Severus at the end of the second century, it is clear that Rome was becoming a military monarchy.

_____9. The acceptance of Christianity by the emperor Galerius may very well have been influenced by his wife.

_____10. A typical approach to understanding reasons for the so-called Fall of Rome is to compare the empire's historical development with the events of the modern Industrial Revolution.

Completion

1. The greatest influence on the cultural development and civilization of Rome during these centuries remained _____ .

2. _____ was the most important of the Augustan poets.

3. _____ was the first Roman emperor whose roots were not among the old Roman nobility.

4. The _____ is the term applied to describe the flowering of Latin literature in the first two centuries of the Christian era.

5. In Greek the word Christos means _____ .

6. The origins of today's Catholic Mass can be found in the ceremonies known in the early Christian era as _____ and _____ .

7. The culture centered in the eastern portions of the late Roman Empire came to be called _____ .

8. In about A.D. 250, the emperor _____ ordered the first major persecution of the Christians.

9. The priest Arius ushered in a long-standing religious controversy by challenging the church's teaching on the _____ .

10. _____ had the power to unite as well as divide.

When

1. When did Vespasian assume the throne?
    (a)   66 CE
    (b)   67 CE
    (c)   68 CE
    (d)   69 CE

2. According to scholars, Jesus was crucified in what year?
    (a)   29 CE
    (b)   30 CE
    (c)   31 CE
    (d)   33 CE

3. In what century was the Roman Empire reorganized and divided, and Christianity came into the forefront?
    (a)   second
    (b)   third
    (c)   fourth
    (d)   none of the above

4. In what century was the demand for romances in literature the most prominent?
    (a)   first
    (b)   second
    (c)   third
    (d)   fourth

5. When did Octavian offer to resign from office?
    (a)   January 13, 27 BCE
    (b)   January 14, 27 BCE
    (c)   January 15, 27 BCE
    (d)   February 13, 27 BCE

Matching

Match the artist to his work.

Cicero	Elegies
Lucretius	treaties on rhetoric, ethics, and politics
Horace	metamorphoses
Propertius	*De Rerum Natura*
Ovid	*Satires*

Map Labeling

Using Map 5-1, answer the following questions by labeling the map accordingly.

1. The territory Trajan added to the empire.

2. In 113-117 CE, which empire did Trajan invade?

3. Trajan also saw the creation of what three eastern provinces?

4. When Hadrian stepped in, what did he do to provide protection (in war) when nature didn't?

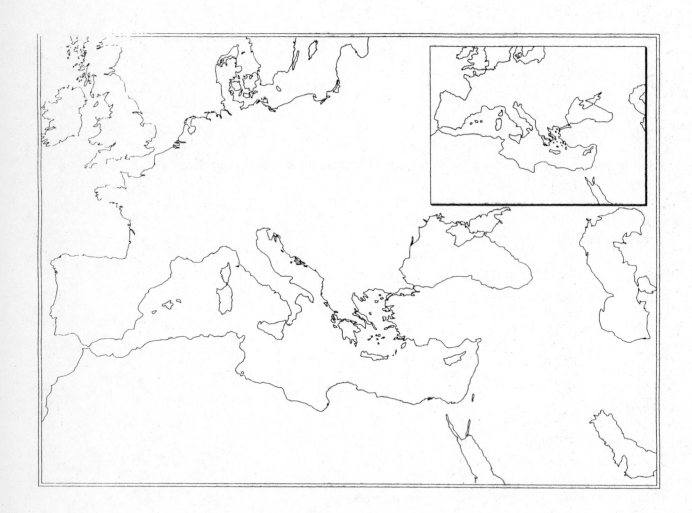

How and Why

1. Describe the political arrangements of the Augustan Principate. How did Augustus deal with the Roman Senate and what effect did this relationship have on the later development of the Empire?

2. Rome was an empire and based its imperial needs on maintaining control of the provinces. What were Rome's policies toward the provinces during this era? Cite specific examples.

3. What were the basic teachings of Jesus of Nazareth? Trace the progress and growth of Christianity from its origins in the first century as an obscure eastern sect to becoming the religion of Rome in the fourth century.

4. With considerable effort, the Roman Empire struggled against internal problems and external threats during the fourth and fifth centuries. In your opinion, if the republic had not been replaced by the empire in the Age of Augustus, could Rome have withstood these later pressures? Discuss your answer fully.

5. Based on your reading and what you have heard in class, what are the causes of the decline and "fall" of the Roman Empire?

Chapter 6
THE EARLY MIDDLE AGES (476-1000): THE BIRTH OF EUROPE

Practice Test

1. The city of _____ was never a center of the government of the Roman Empire.
   (a) Naples
   (b) Milan
   (c) Ravenna
   (d) Constantinople

2. Who urged monds to focus more on caring for the needy than on personal asceticism?
   (a) Anthony of Egypt
   (b) Pachomius
   (c) Athanasius
   (d) Basil the Great

3. Which of the following is the least correct about the practice of the Islamic faith?
   (a) Charity is forbidden.
   (b) Polygamy is permitted.
   (c) Eating pork is forbidden.
   (d) There is no clear distinction between the clergy and the laity.

4. Originally, persons who became monks were
   (a) both men and women.
   (b) hermits.
   (c) Sophists.
   (d) converted Muslims.

5. Life on a manor consisted of all of the following except:
   (a) security.
   (b) communal farming.
   (c) dividing harvests equally.
   (d) living off what one grew on the land.

6. The Papal States was a region in
   (a) Northern Italy.
   (b) Southern Italy.
   (c) Western Italy.
   (d) Central Italy .

7. Which of the following is the most accurate statement about the feudal system?
    (a) Serfs spent most of the week working the lord's fields.
    (b) The scratch plow was an   improvement over the moldboard plow.
    (c) All peasants (serfs) were equal.
    (d) Records show that peasants attempted to escape the system.

8. Which of the following brothers was not involved in the settlement known as the Treaty of Verdun?
    (a) Pepin
    (b) Charles the Bald
    (c) Louis the German
    (d) Lothar

9. Probably the darkest period of this era was
    (a) the latter part of the eighth century.
    (b) the ninth century.
    (c) the last quarter of the ninth century and the first half of the tenth century.
    (d) all of the above

10. The word *vassal* derives from a term meaning
    (a) those who serve.
    (b) tenement.
    (c) monetary payment.
    (d) freemen in a contractual relation of dependence.

True-False

_____1. By the fifth century A.D., the city of Constantinople was in effect the "New Rome."

_____ 2. Germans never held command posts in the Roman army.

_____3. The 378 A.D., battle at Adrianople saw the Roman Emperor Valens defeated by the Visigoths.

_____4. Byzantine clergymen frequently supported popular entertainment modes, especially the theater.

_____5. Byzantine civilization, until its fall in the fifteenth century, provided an excellent example of civilized society.

_____6. The word Islam means, "partisans of Ali."

_____ 7.   Charlemagne's oldest son, by his second marriage, launched an ill-fated campaign against his father.

_____ 8.   One of the major issues separating the Eastern and Western churches was the adoption by the West of the so-called filiogue clause, making Christ "fully substantial with God the Father."

_____ 9.   Charles Martel was Charlemagne's father.

_____ 10. In feudal terminology, a "liege lord" was the individual to whom a particular vassal owed the most money.

Completion

1. Despite the controversy involved, the Monophysites were supported by the Empress _____ .

2. _____ was a major pilgrimage site for Muhammad and his followers.

3. One of the key events in Muhammad's life was his flight from Mecca to Medina, which is known to Muslims as the _____ .

4. Islam's greatest authority on Aristotle, this philosopher is known in the West as _____ .

5. The father of hermit monasticism was _____ .

6. The concept of _____ held that the authority of the Bishop of Rome was unassailable.

7. The founder of the Merovingian dynasty was _____ .

8. Charles Martel's 732 A.D. victory at _____ ended Arab expansion into Western Europe.

9. The eighth-century Anglo-Saxon scholar _____ was the person responsible for bringing classical and Christian learning to Charlemagne's palace school at Aachen.

10. During the Middle Ages a land grant was called a_____ or _____ .

When

1. When did the Visigoths sack Rome?
    (a) 370
    (b) 409
    (c) 410
    (d) 455

2. Charlemagne's reign lasted from
    (a) 527-566.
    (b) 622-732.
    (c) 751-768.
    (d) 768-814.

3. A new type of plow that aided workers in tilling the soil came about during which era?
    (a) Dark Ages
    (b) Carolignian
    (c) Byantine
    (d) none of the above

4. Constantinople fell to the Turks in what year?
    (a) 1500
    (b) 1476
    (c) 1525
    (d) 1453

5. When were the "reveal texts" that God gave to Muhammad assembled into the Qur'an?
    (a) between 500 and 501
    (b) between 600 and 620
    (c) between 650 and 651
    (d) between 750 and 751

Matching

Match the part of the *Corpus Juris Civilis* with the law it focused on

Code	Justinian's decrees
Institutes	revised imperial edits
Novellae	textbook for training authors
Digest	summarized opinions of famous legal experts

Map Labeling

Using Map 6-3, answer the following questions by labeling the map accordingly:

1. What was the pope the secular ruler of?

2. Which island did Charlemagne rule near the time of his death?

3. Charlemagne constructed a castle in which city?

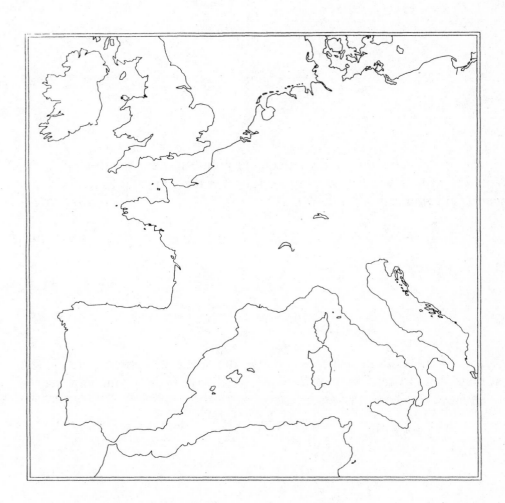

How and Why

1. What were the chief issues that divided the Eastern church (Constantinople) and the Western church (Rome)?

2. Explain the basic characteristics of the Islamic faith. Why were the Muslims able to expand so rapidly?

3. Describe the political, social, economic, and intellectual life in Europe at the time of Charlemagne. Would you say that these descriptions reflected the values of Roman civilization or that of Christianity?

4. Discuss the problems of the Carolingian succession after the death of Charlemagne. How did these problems lead to the Treaty of Verdun? What have been the modern implications of this treaty?

5. Describe in detail what you consider the key factors in the transition of Western Europe from the Roman Empire to the early Middle Ages.

Chapter 7
THE HIGH MIDDLE AGES (1000–1300):
THE ASCENDENCY OF THE CHURCH AND THE RISE OF STATES

Practice Test

1. Which of the following most accurately describes Western European progress and development during the High Middle Ages?
   - (a) a growing independence of the Roman church from secular authority
   - (b) the establishment of national monarchies
   - (c) the foundations for modern representative institutions
   - (d) all of the above

2. The relationship between Otto the Great and the papacy at Rome can best be described as
   - (a) Otto's domination of the popes.
   - (b) papal domination of the German monarchy.
   - (c) a near-perfect balance in their respective authorities.
   - (d) none of the above

3. All of the following were the principles of the reformers of Cluny EXCEPT
   - (a) rejection of secular control of the clergy.
   - (b) strict observance of monastic rules.
   - (c) creation of a more spiritual Church.
   - (d) acceptance of life without hope.

4. The purpose of the College of Cardinals was to
   - (a) establish educational standards for the clergy.
   - (b) free the papacy from secular intervention.
   - (c) provide an internal organization for Church discipline.
   - (d) none of the above

5. Lay investiture could best be described as a process
   - (a) by which the College of Cardinals appointed bishops.
   - (b) by which a layperson appointed someone to church office.
   - (c) in which Henry IV begged forgiveness before Gregory VII.
   - (d) fully accepted by the Cluniac Reform Movement.

6. Which of the following would <u>not</u> be considered a contribution to the success of the First Crusade?
   - (a) the need to arouse the European Christian community
   - (b) the romance of a pilgrimage to the Holy Land
   - (c) promises of a plenary indulgence
   - (d) wide-spread popular support for the reformed papacy

7. During this period, the person most responsible for raising the prestige of the church was
    (a) Saint Francis.
    (b) Saint Louis.
    (c) Pope Hadrian IV.
    (d) Pope Innocent III.

8. What spurred on the Battle of Hastings?
    (a) the usurpation of the throne by Harold Godwinsson
    (b) William of Normandy's desire to be king
    (c) the death of Edward the confessor
    (d) none of the above

9. _____ were each married to Eleanor of Aquitaine.
    (a) William the Conqueror and Henry II
    (b) Louis VII and Henry II
    (c) Richard the Lion-Hearted and King John
    (d) Louis VII and Henry I

10. The so-called Sicilian Connection led to
    (a) papal control of all of Italy.
    (b) an alliance between Henry VI and Innocent III.
    (c) repeated German attempts to control Sicily
    (d) a general European war.

True-False

_____1. The belief in separation of church and state began during the High Middle Ages.

_____2. A demand for celibacy was an important driving force of the Cluniac Reform Movement.

_____3. Greed was the chief inspiration for the early Crusades.

_____4. During this period of history, Bernard of Clairvaux was probably the most influential monastic leader.

_____5. The Fourth Lateran Council formalized the sacrament of Penance (Reconciliation) as a central means of religious discipline.

_____6. An early symbol of the resistance to monarchial authority can be found in the story of the assassination of Thomas à Becket.

_____7. In a discussion of the impact of the Magna Carta, the peculiar political genius of the English should be considered above all else.

_____8. The French king Louis IX's successes at home and abroad can be considered the result of his religious fanaticism.

_____9. The German king Frederick I's efforts against Arnold of Brescia restored Pope Adrian IV's position in Italy.

_____10. Between 1250 and 1272 the Hohenstaufen dynasty slowly faded into oblivion.

Completion

1. In the tenth century, Otto the Great's father, _____ , placed his son in a strong territorial position.

2. One of the first popes to reign without the consent of the Holy Roman Emperor was _____ .

3. In 1122, the Investiture Controversy was apparently settled in the agreements of the _____ .

4. Pope _____ sponsored the First Crusade.

5. _____ was the most important church meeting of this period.

6. One of the greatest medieval thinkers, _____ was the leading theologian of the Dominican Order.

7. In winning the battle of _____ , William the Conqueror made good his claim to the English throne.

8. William the Conqueror's exact survey of England is known as the _____.

9. _____ was the most powerful and successful of the French monarchs during this era.

10. _____ organized the German princes against Frederick who were a superior force and able to gain full control of Germany by the 1240s.

When

1. In what century did Christians eventually come to believe in the doctrine transubstantiation?
    (a)   tenth
    (b)   eleventh
    (c)   twelfth
    (d)   thirteenth

2. In what year was the Franciscan Order founded?
    (a)   1208
    (b)   1210
    (c)   1216
    (d)   1220

3. In what year was the Treaty of Paris negotiated?
    (a)   1159
    (b)   1212
    (c)   1259
    (d)   1279

4. In what year was King John obliged to recognize the Magna Carta?
    (a)   1115
    (b)   1215
    (c)   1315
    (d)   1415

5. During what span of time was Eleanor of Aquitaine kept under house arrest?
    (a)   1169-1179
    (b)   1179-1189
    (c)   1279-1389
    (d)   1280-1291

Matching

Match the individual to the accomplishment or characteristic are the most noted for.

Innocent	the embodiment of a perfect ruler
Henry II	creation of Franciscians and Dominicans
Louis IX	canonization of Francis of Assisi
Frederick II	the creation of the English-French empire
Pope Gregory IX	ended Otto IVs treacherous reign

Map Labeling

Use the map on page 167 of the textbook, to answer the questions below. Label the map accordingly.

1. Otto IV attacked what city, which lead to his excommunication by Pope Innocent III?

2. In what city was Frederick II crowned king?

3. In what city did Frederick mount the throne?

4. Where did Frederick grow up?

5. Frederick's chief political objective was to win control of what area?

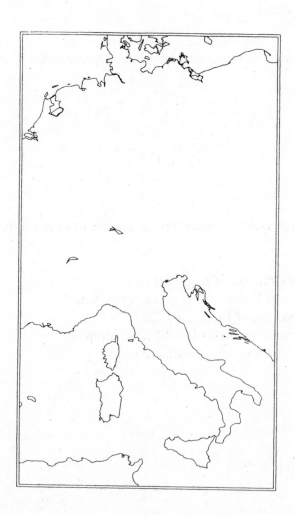

How and Why

1. How did the Lay Investiture controversy of the eleventh century reflect the medieval situation of church-state relations?

2. What were the causes of the Crusades? Were they successful? Describe the overall effect of the Crusades on Western Europe.

3. Compare and contrast the internal political development of England and France from the mid-eleventh to the mid-thirteenth century. Cite examples as necessary.

4. Compare the pontificate of Innocent III with the reigns of secular rulers in the thirteenth century. How would you assess Innocent's achievements on behalf of the church in relation to achievements of secular rulers on behalf of the state?

5. Discuss the reign of Frederick II. In your opinion, did he have any strength as a ruler?

Chapter 8
THE HIGH MIDDLE AGES (100–1300):
PEOPLE, TOWNS, AND UNIVERSITIES

Practice Test

1. The pastimes of the medieval nobility during the Middle Ages were dominated by
    (a) card playing and gambling.
    (b) fishing and drinking.
    (c) hunting and tournaments.
    (d) tournaments and carousing.

2. Courtly love can be described by each of the following EXCEPT
    (a) love at a distance.
    (b) sex without physical contact.
    (c) lovers who always suffered the consequences.
    (d) love unconsummated by sexual intercourse.

3. As contrasted with the secular clergy, the regular clergy of the Middle Ages could best be described as
    (a) the least prayerful among the clergy.
    (b) the spiritual elite among the clergy.
    (c) the least respected among the clergy.
    (d) composed of churchmen above the rank of bishop.

4. All of the following improved agricultural productivity for peasants EXCEPT
    (a) the horse collar.
    (b) the discovery of corn.
    (c) the horseshoe.
    (d) crop rotation.

5. In order to earn a bachelor's degree, students had to master
    (a) arithmetic.
    (b) music.
    (c) rhetoric.
    (d) astronomy.

6. The Summa Theologica was written by
    (a) John of Salisbury.
    (b) William of Ockham.
    (c) Peter Lombard.
    (d) none of the above

7. Berengar of Tours was a medieval scholastic who questioned the church's teaching on
   (a) monasticism.
   (b) clerical celibacy.
   (c) the Trinity.
   (d) transubstantiation.

8. In this era, nunneries, our modem convents, provided a place
   (a) of refuge for a sinful woman.
   (b) for women to learn blue-collar trades.
   (c) to obtain an education.
   (d) none of the above

9. The image of women in medieval society might best be described as
   (a) taken from Adam's side.
   (b) contradictory.
   (c) man's partner in life.
   (d) none of the above apply

10. Medieval children
   (a) are now considered to have been more highly regarded than once thought.
   (b) assumed adult responsibilities at an early age.
   (c) usually began schooling or apprenticing at the age of eight.
   (d) all of the above

True-False

_____1. While the nobility viewed warfare as the natural state of things, townspeople and peasants preferred peace.

_____2. The evolution of the modern concept of courtesy originally stems from the social problems created by the nobility.

_____3. During this period of European history it is estimated that as much as 15 percent of the population were clerics.

_____4. It is noted that by the eleventh century, only about 5 percent of the population lived in an urban setting.

_____5. Medieval Jews were distrusted and persecuted because of their financial influence and from the influence of established church teachings.

_____6. Thanks to the Muslim scholars of Spain, many of the works of the classical era Greeks were preserved and often translated into Latin.

_____7. The church whole-heartedly embraced Scholasticism.

_____8.   Strict laws were enforced concerning the number of manors a lord could hold.

_____9.   In the Middle Ages, impoverished knights were known as "weaker vessels."

_____10. Chattel slaves and peasants had very similar lifestyles.

Completion

1. The ceremonial entrance into the noble class was called _____ .

2. The once great power of the _____ declined as a result of several factors ranging from loss of population to changes in military tactics during the fourteenth century.

3. Though medieval lords were probably less severe in their control over the serfs than we might think, they had the right to exact what we might call today nuisance taxes, known as _____ .

4. Within the medieval cities, competing _____ developed primarily to enhance the business interest of their members.

5. An alliance developed between _____ and _____ because both wanted strong central governments for nation-states.

6. The first important Western university was founded at _____ .

7. The _____ of the early universities gave them a unique independence.

8. The college system first developed at the University of _____ .

9. The standard textbook for medieval theology was Peter Lombard's _____ .

10. Germanic codes recognized the rights of women to _____, _____, _____, and _____ family property and personal possessions.

When

1. Merchant guilds began to appear on the scene in which century?
   (a) tenth
   (b) eleventh
   (c) twelfth
   (d) thirteenth

2. Students typically entered the university between the ages of
   - (a) 11 and 15
   - (b) 12 and 16
   - (c) 12 and 15
   - (d) 11 and 16

3. What changed European warfare during the eighth century?
   - (a) lances
   - (b) armed merchants
   - (c) the rifle
   - (d) stirrups

4. During medieval times, around half of the population's children died before the age of
   - (a) 4.
   - (b) 5.
   - (c) 6.
   - (d) 7.

5. The nobility saw their power as a class decline in which century?
   - (a) twelfth
   - (b) thirteenth
   - (c) fourteenth
   - (d) fifteenth

Matching

Match each group of people with their service during medieval society.

Knights	land workers
Clergy	work among the laity
Peasants	production of supplies
Village artisans	protection
Secular clergy	prayer intervention

Map Labeling

Using Map 8-1 (p. 178) answer the following questions.

1. In what area could you find spices?

2. If you wanted to purchase fur, where would you travel to?

3. Olive oil was typically found in _____.

4. You could purchase honey near which cities?

5. Slaves and grain were near what city?

How and Why

1. As you imagine it, describe what medieval life was like for each of the four social classes: nobility, clergy, townspeople, and peasants.

2. Describe a typical diet of this era. Plan a weekly menu for an average thirteenth-century peasant. How might this menu vary for a contemporary nobleman's family or that of a townsman?

3. Based on your understanding of the medieval experience, what suggestions would you make for improving or changing higher education today?

4. How would you assess the position of women within each of the classes of medieval society? How were their roles and functions similar to, and different from, those of women in previous ages and those of women in modern times?

5. Describe the life of children in this period of the Middle Ages. Compare and contrast with modern theories of child rearing, and with your own views.

Chapter 9
THE LATE MIDDLE AGES (1300–1527): CENTURIES OF CRISIS

Practice Test

1. The three great calamities developed in this chapter are
    (a) civil war in England, the Jacquerie in France, and the Hussite revolt in the empire.
    (b) the circumstances surrounding the execution of Joan of Arc, midterm exams, and the Lollard revolt in England.
    (c) basically war, plague, and schism.
    (d) all of the above

2. The longbow was an effective weapon because it could
    (a) reach considerable distances.
    (b) fire six arrows a minute when properly manned.
    (c) pierce armor.
    (d) all of the above capabilities existed

3. In reality, the success of Joan of Arc was caused by
    (a) divine intervention.
    (b) her military genius.
    (c) her youth.
    (d) her inspiration.

4. One of the outcomes of the Hundred Years' War was that the French region of _____ became a major European political power.
    (a) Normandy
    (b) Burgundy
    (c) Lyon
    (d) the Isle de France

5. As a result of the Black Death, it is estimated that the western European population was reduced by
    (a) 40 percent.
    (b) 50 percent.
    (c) 60 percent.
    (d) 70 percent.

6. Avignon is located in
    (a) France.
    (b) Italy.
    (c) Germany.
    (d) England.

7. The statement that the clergy "ought to be content with food and clothing" is associated with
    (a) John Wycliffe.
    (b) Pope John XXII.
    (c) John Huss.
    (d) John Ziska.

8. The basic argument of the conciliarists was that
    (a) church councils working with the pope were best suited to lead the faithful.
    (b) church councils guided and directed by a nonschismatic pope would be best.
    (c) church legislation could only be decided through a series of regionally sponsored councils.
    (d) none of the above

9 Which of the following statements is the <u>least</u> correct concerning the Council of Constance?
    (a) A decree was issued that said councils were the ultimate source of authority in the church.
    (b) In 1958, Pope John XXIII declared this council to be the greatest ever convened.
    (c) The Council made provisions for subsequent meetings on a regular basis.
    (d) It elected Martin V as the pope.

10. The Black Death first appeared in
    (a) Venice.
    (b) Genoa.
    (c) Sicily.
    (d) Pisa.

True-False

_____1.   Joan of Arc was canonized a saint in 1456.

_____2.   The greatest famine of the Middle Ages occurred just prior to the Black Death, and can be considered among the important causes of this plague.

_____3.   As the Black Death took its grim toll in Europe, it should be noted that townspeople and the church profited.

_____4.   Celestine V, a Calabrian hermit, can be described as a saintly, but inept pope.

_____5.   The papal bull of 1301 "Listen, My Son," allowed continued taxation of the clergy in France.

_____6.   The so-called Gallican liberties permitted wide governmental control of taxation and ecclesiastical appointments in France.

_____7.   John Ziska was an important Hussite leader in the first half of the fifteenth century.

_____8.   The declaration Sacrosancta was considered the authoritative basis of the Conciliar Movement.

_____9.   Prince Vladimir turned Kiev into a wonderful political and cultural center that rivaled Constantinople.

_____10.   The words crisis and calamity may be commonly used to describe the late medieval period of Western history.

Completion

1. In this period, the development of the _____ gave England a clear military advantage against the French.

2. During the early stages of the Hundred Years' War, France experienced a widespread popular revolt known as the _____ .

3. France saw considerable territorial devastation during the war, but experienced the awakening of _____.

4. An excellent source for understanding how people reacted to the great plague of the fourteenth century can be found in Boccaccio's _____ .

5. The struggle between Philip IV of France and Pope Boniface VIII is symbolic of the struggle for political power between _____ and _____ in the late Middle Ages.

6. _____ believed the pope had no special powers of infallibility.

7. Founded in the mid-fourteenth century, the _____ was a center for religious reform and for a growing Czech nationalism.

8. Granted an audience at the Council of Constance, _____ was executed there for heresy in the summer of 1415.

9. The papal bull _____ could be considered the final blow to the Conciliar Movement.

10. After the death of Yaroslav the Wise, Russian people were divided into _____, _____, and _____ .

When

1. In what month and year did Joan of Arc appear in Charles's court in exile?
    (a) February 1329
    (b) March 1329
    (c) January 1429
    (d) March 1429

2. During thirty-five years of life in the late Middle Ages, an individual could expect to experience an education in
   (a) war.
   (b) hunger.
   (c) education.
   (d) none of the above

3. In what year did Ghengis Khan invade Russia?
   (a) 1221
   (b) 1223
   (c) 1232
   (d) 1240

4. Which of the following sequence of church councils is in proper chronological order?
   (a) Pisa, Basel, Constance
   (b) Basel, Pisa, Constance
   (c) Constance, Basel, Pisa
   (d) Pisa, Constance, Basel

5. Which reflects the correct order of events?
   (a) Battle of Crecy and seizure of Calais; Treaty of Troyes; Joan of Arc executed
   (b) Avignon Papacy; Joan of Arc executed; Black Death strikes
   (c) English Peasants Revolt; Black Death; End of the Hundred Years' War
   (d) Black Death strikes; English Peasants Revolt; Battle of Crecy and seizure of Calais

Matching

Match the pope to what he was known for.

Gregory XI   sold indulgences
Clement V   excommunicated William of Ockham
Clement VI   agreed to move the papacy from Avignon to Rome
John XXII   began construction of a palace at Avignon
Benedict XII   increased papal taxation of the clergy

Map Labeling

Using Map 9-1, label the following inset maps accordingly.

1. Which port did Edward seize?

2. Where did the English win their greatest victory?

3. Where was the Battle of Agincourt fought?

4. What city was Joan of Arc told to rescue?

5. By the end of the war, England clung to a little territory around what port?

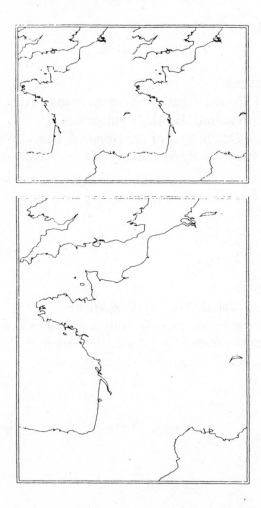

How and Why

1. Discuss the causes, events, and significance of the Hundred Years' War. Estimate how this war affected the townspeople and peasants in both England and France. Were people affected differently in each country?

2. Describe what you consider to be the urban and rural effects of the Black Death.

3. What were the causes and effects of the Great Schism? How does the Conciliar Movement relate to the Great Schism?

4. Who were the Hussites? What were their fundamental principles? To what extent did the church willingly make concessions to this movement? In your opinion, what Hussite practices/positions have made their way into modern church practices, Catholic or Protestant?

5. Give an overall assessment of these two centuries from the perspective of (1) economic progress, (2) social change, and (3) key developments within the Roman Catholic Church, especially those considered to be of far-reaching consequence.

Chapter 10
RENAISSANCE AND DISCOVERY

Practice Test

1. Florence evolved into a Renaissance city by displaying WHICH the following characteristics?
    (a) the old rich
    (b) an emerging merchant class
    (c) middle-burgher ranks and the little people
    (d) all of the above

2. For Europe the late fifteenth and sixteenth centuries were a period that saw
    (a) the collapse of the Atlantic slave trade.
    (b) unprecedented territorial growth and ideological experimentation.
    (c) successful curtailing of ideas by the church.
    (d) a continued weakening of the European trade system.

3. Which of the following was NOT written by Francesco Petrarch?
    (a) *Letters to the Ancient Dead*
    (b) *Vita Nuova*
    (c) *Africa*
    (d) *Lives of Illustrious Men*

4. The Renaissance center for Platonist and Neoplatonist thought was the city of
    (a) Florence.
    (b) Rome.
    (c) Paris.
    (d) Venice.

5. The Renaissance gave a new perspective to life which is probably best evidenced in
    (a) warfare.
    (b) music and literature.
    (c) painting and sculpture.
    (d) education and philosophy.

6. Renaissance paintings appeared three-dimensional as a result of
    (a) adjustments to the size of the figures portrayed.
    (b) the use of shading.
    (c) the use of oil paints.
    (d) all of the above

7. _____ is considered the most corrupt pope of all times.
    (a) Julius II
    (b) Innocent III
    (c) John XXIII
    (d) Alexander VI

8. Which of the following figures would be considered the least responsible for the fall of the Italian city-states during this period?
    (a) Machiavelli
    (b) Ferdinand of Aragon
    (c) Ludovico il Moro
    (d) Charles VIII.

9. Machiavelli's *The Prince* was dedicated to
    (a) Holy Roman Emperor Charles V.
    (b) Lorenzo de' Medici.
    (c) Lorenzo the Magnificent.
    (d) Pope Clement VII.

10. The creation of an electoral college for the Holy Roman Empire can be found in the
    (a) Imperial Council of Regency.
    (b) Golden Bull of 1356.
    (c) Assembly at Worms.
    (d) none of the above

True-False

_____1.   Within the divisions of Florentine society in the Renaissance era, the popolo minuto were viewed as the highest.

_____2.   Authorities have a firm definition of the term *humanism*.

_____3.   The father of Renaissance painting was Giotto.

_____4.   Surprisingly, Michelangelo's famous statue of David is only eight feet high.

_____5.   In the fifteenth century, the imperial diet was a ceremonial meal taken by several German princes publicly in the Reichstag.

_____ 6.   During the late Middle Ages, the number of universities in Europe doubled.

_____7.   Johann Reuchlin invented the printing press.

_____8.   Study of original versions of early Christian literature, a call for simple piety, and a disciplined study of the Bible are virtues said to have been encouraged by Desiderius Erasmus.

_____9.   The 1516 work *Utopia* by Thomas More suggested a distinct division of social classes and personal property would make for an ideal society.

_____10. The Aztecs believed that the gods must literally be fed with human bodies to guarantee continuing sunshine and soil fertility.

Completion

1. _____ remained an oligarchic republic while the other city-states in Italy were run by despots.

2. The works of _____ and _____ are said to form the basis of the Italian vernacular language.

3. _____ was an influential book which stressed the importance of integrating knowledge of language and history with other skills while calling for good manners and high moral character.

4. The Donation of Constantine was a fraudulent document that had supported church claims to vast territories in Italy, but was exposed in the fifteenth century by the humanist scholar _____ .

5. _____ was a fresco portraying the great minds of Western philosophy.

6. The English Parliament, the Spanish Cortes, and the French _____ are all considered evolving representative assemblies.

7. The unification of Spain was effected by the marriage in 1469 of Isabella of _____ to Ferdinand of _____.

8. The greatest Christian Humanist of this era was _____.

9. _____ was Europe's foremost authority on Jewish learning before his death in 1522.

10. Though not fully matured, there is growing evidence that the economic foundation of Western European life today in the form of _____.

When

1. In what year did Cosimo de' Medici take charge of Florence?
    (a) 1430
    (b) 1434
    (c) 1439
    (d) 1534

2. In what century did the high Renaissance blossom?
    (a) fourteenth
    (b) late fifteenth
    (c) late sixteenth
    (d) early fourteenth

3. Which is the correct order of events?
    (a) Louis XII invades Italy; Treaty of Lodi; Francis I invades Italy
    (b) Francis I invades Italy; Treaty of Lodi; Louis XII invades Italy
    (c) Treaty of Lodi; Louis XII invades Italy; Francis I invades Italy
    (d) Treaty of Lodi; Rome sacked by imperial soldiers; Francis I invades Italy

4. In what year was Thomas More executed?
    (a) 1520
    (b) 1525
    (c) 1530
    (d) 1535

5. When did Da Gama reach India?
    (a) 1496
    (b) 1497
    (c) 1498
    (d) 1499

Matching

Match the author to his/her most famous piece of work.

Petrarch	*Education of the Orator*
Dante Alighieri	*The City of Ladies*
Boccaccio	*Letters to the Ancient Dead*
Christine de Pisan	*Decameron*
Quintilian	*Divine Comedy*

Map Labeling

Use Map 10-2 to answer the following questions.

1. From which city did the Portuguese import gold?

2. Where did Columbus set sail from on his first voyage?

3. When did Magellan set off to navigate the globe?

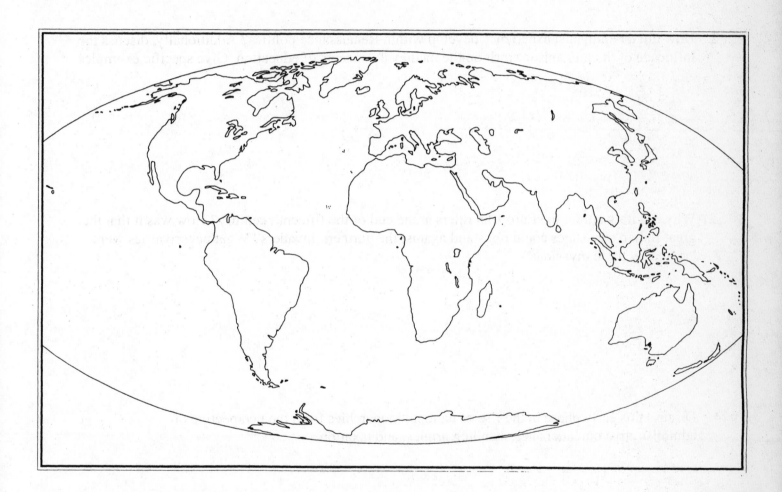

How and Why

1. Give a complete definition of humanism. Describe key humanistic ideas within the context of the Renaissance. What is the debate over Jacob Burckhart's nineteenth-century description of this era?

2. How did the humanist experience develop within Renaissance politics? Additionally, discuss the influence of the humanistic spirit on the medieval concepts of education. Give specific examples.

3. Why did Italy attract the European rulers at the end of the fifteenth century? How was it that the great Italian city-states could not stand against the northern invaders? What new rivalries were created by these invasions?

4. Discuss this early phase in the rise of national monarchies from the perspective of administrative bureaucracies, standing armies, and taxation.

5. Mindful of this quincentenary era (1492–1992) of Columbus' landing in the Americas, described the initial contact between the Europeans and the Amer-Indians they encountered. Is there a pattern to these encounters? Over the centuries since that time, what has been the historic view of Europe's discovery of the "New World"?

Chapter 11
THE AGE OF REFORMATION

Practice Test

1. Brothers of the Common Life were noted for
    - (a) their work in schools.
    - (b) their work as copyists.
    - (c) running hospices.
    - (d) all of the above

2. The concept of indulgences was based upon a concept described by Pope Clement VI as drawn from
    - (a) Crusades to the Holy Land.
    - (b) treasury of merit.
    - (c) letters of indulgence.
    - (d) sufferings in purgatory.

3. By studying _____ letters, Luther gained the insight and peace he needed concerning the process of salvation.
    - (a) St. John
    - (b) St. Luke
    - (c) St. Paul
    - (d) St. Matthew

4. In his _____, Luther argued that only two of the seven sacraments were necessary for salvation.
    - (a) ninety five theses
    - (b) Freedom of a Christian
    - (c) Babylonian Captivity of the Church
    - (d) Address to the Christian Nobility of the German Nation

5. Which of the following practices did Zwingli question and repudiate in the course of his reforms?
    - (a) fasting and the worship of saints
    - (b) transubstantiation
    - (c) pilgrimages and clerical celibacy
    - (d) all of the above

6. All of the following EXCEPT one were Spiritualists.
    - (a) Thomas Muntzer
    - (b) Michael Servetus
    - (c) Sebastian Franck
    - (d) Caspar Schwenckfeld

7. The reform efforts of the Council of Trent included all of the following EXCEPT
   (a) several doctrinal concessions to the reformers.
   (b) restored internal church discipline.
   (c) reform of the office of bishop.
   (d) increased respect of the parish priest.

8. With regard to changes in educational attitudes during the sixteenth century, Protestantism
   (a) rejected humanism.
   (b) supported all humanistic positions.
   (c) replaced humanism with Protestant scholasticism.
   (d) generally endorsed humanism.

9. Generally speaking, Protestant thinkers viewed women as
   (a) temptresses.
   (b) bores.
   (c) models of the Virgin Mary.
   (d) companions.

10. William Shakespeare was believed to be all of the following except:
   (a) playwright
   (b) actor
   (c) director
   (d) owner-producer of plays

True-False

_____1.   The Reformation started in Germany and Switzerland.

_____2.   Turkish attacks in the eastern empire and several wars against France in Italy managed to distract Charles V as the Protestant Reformation began in earnest.

_____3.   Martin Luther supported the German Peasants' Revolt of 1524–25.

_____4.   Ulrich Zwingli opposed each of the following: mercenary service, religious superstition, and the sale of indulgences.

_____5.   Zwingli and Luther held similar beliefs about the nature of Christ's presence in the Eucharist.

_____6.   It has been estimated that between the years 1525 and 1618 between 1,000 and 5,000 men and women were executed for rebaptizing themselves as adults.

_____7.   It is said that the signing of the 1552 Peace of Passau gained the Emperor Charles V's lifelong ambition to maintain religious unity in Europe.

_____8.   "If a man takes his brother's wife, they shall be without children," appears in Leviticus 20, and was a serious admonition against Henry VIII's first marriage.

_____9.   Unlike the previous great church councils of the later Middle Ages, the Council of Trent was dominated by Italian clerics.

_____10.   *Don Quixote* tell the true tale of a deluded knight.

Completion

1. A prime example in the development of lay religious movements in the late Middle Ages was the _____ .

2. _____ was probably the most popularly read book of the pre-Reformation era.

3. In 1512, Martin Luther received a Doctorate in Theology from the University of _____ .

4. An end to clerical celibacy was an important argument in the reforms of _____ .

5. The person associated with the advent of Anabaptism was _____.

6. The advisor to Henry VIII who failed to secure the annulment for him was _____ .

7. The official document that made the reigning monarch of England head of the church there was _____ .

8. The Council of _____ was a most important effort in the church's Counter-Reformation.

9. Generally, Protestant reforms had the effect of reducing the medieval concept of the distinction between the clergy and the _____.

10. Protestant teachings had a definite effect upon the role of _____ in society.

When

1. When did Luther post his 95 theses on the door of Castle Church?
   (a)   October 1, 1517
   (b)   October 31, 1517
   (c)   November 1, 1517
   (d)   November 31, 1517

2. How long was Luther in hiding for his said crime of heresy?
   (a) 1 year
   (b) 1.5 years
   (c) 2 years
   (d) none of the above

3. Among contenders for the Imperial crown of the Holy Roman Empire after the death of Maximilian I were
    (a) Francis I of France and Charles I of Spain.
    (b) Henry VIII of England and Catherine of Aragon.
    (c) Charles V of Germany and Jacob Fugger of Augsburg.
    (d) none of the above

4. In what decade was the Society of Jesus organized?
   (a) 1490s
   (b) 1500s
   (c) 1520s
   (d) 1530s

5. In what year did Cervantes begin to write *Don Quixote*?
   (a) 1600
   (b) 1601
   (c) 1602
   (d) 1603

Matching

Below are listed five of Henry the VIII's wives. Match the wife to the fate and/or purpose of each one's marriage to Henry.

Anne Boleyn	beheaded for adultery
Jane Seymour	a patron of humanists and reforms—outlived Henry
Anne of Cleves	charge with treason and adultery and was beheaded
Catherine Howard	forged an alliance among Protestant princes
Catherine Parr	gave Henry a male heir—Edward

Map Labeling

Using Map 11-2, identify which cities: Geneva, Rome, Vienna, Wittenberg, and Bavaria, were under control of the following religious groups. Label the map.

Lutheran   Anabaptist   Calvinist control

Anglican   Roman Catholic

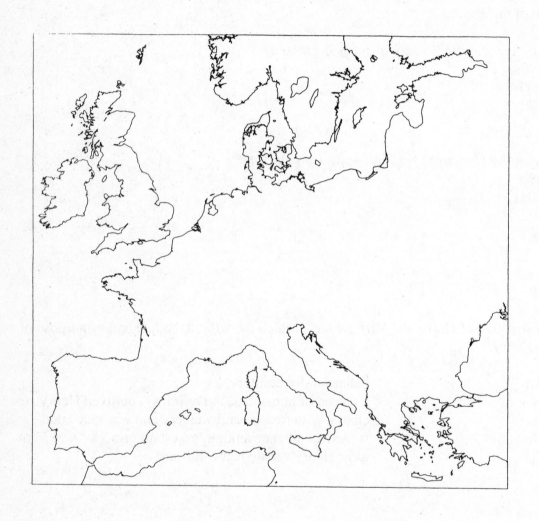

How and Why

1. Assess religious attitudes in Europe before Luther. Were these views related to the weakness of the papacy and the church organization at the time or were other factors involved? Explain your answer fully.

2. Describe Calvin's life and the times through which he lived. How would you assess his role as ruler of Geneva? What has been the impact of Calvin's teachings in Europe? In America?

3. Protestant radicalism was well entrenched by the end of the sixteenth century despite efforts by Catholics and other Protestant denominations to stop the spread. Describe several of these radical religious philosophies. What effect, if any, did they have on the Reformation?

4. How would you describe the overall impact of the Protestant Reformation upon sixteenth-century Europe? How did the rise of Protestantism permanently alter the course of Western civilization?

5. Having studied the last several chapters on the doctrines of the Roman Catholic Church as well as those of the various Protestant reformers, could you envision the possibility that a religious settlement could be reached in our time by which the Christian faith would again be one?

Chapter 12
THE AGE OF RELIGIOUS WARS

Practice Test

1. Which of the following is the most accurate statement about the Counter-Reformation?
   (a) The church emerged with an organizational structure emphasizing absolute obedience to the person at the top.
   (b) Catholics were permitted by the Church to convert to Lutheranism under the Augsburg Settlement.
   (c) The Roman Church adopted a Presbyterian organization structure.
   (d) none of the above

2. Huguenotism, or French Calvinism, was normally supported by
   (a) a majority of the population.
   (b) mainly the lower classes.
   (c) almost all the French nobility.
   (d) none of the above

3. Which of the following was not a work supporting the Protestant concept of defense?
   (a) Doctrine of Amboise
   (b) Blast of the Trumpet Against the Terrible Regiment of Women
   (c) On the Right of Magistrates over Their Subjects
   (d) Defense of Liberty Against Tyrants

4. The phrase, "Paris is worth a mass," is attributed to
   (a) Catherine de Médici.
   (b) Gaspard de Coligny.
   (c) Henry of Navarre.
   (d) Henry III..

5. In the 1560s, _____ brutally suppressed a Protestant uprising in the Netherlands.
   (a) William of Orange
   (b) Duke of Alba
   (c) Cardinal Granvelle
   (d) Don John of Austria

6. Compared with her half-sister and successor Elizabeth, Mary I's repression of Protestantism in England is considered to be
   (a) about the same.
   (b) more selective.
   (c) greater by far.
   (d) a model of forbearance.

7. Most sixteenth-century Puritans were
    (a) Congregationalists.
    (b) Anglicans.
    (c) Presbyterians.
    (d) Catholics.

8. From Elizabeth I's point of view, the dilemma caused by Mary, Queen of Scots was essentially that she was
    (a) Catholic.
    (b) Elizabeth's legitimate successor and determined to displace her.
    (c) personally jealous of Elizabeth.
    (d) more attractive than Elizabeth.

9. The invading fleet of the Spanish Armada was composed of approximately _____ ships.
    (a) 75
    (b) 130
    (c) 180
    (d) 230

10. The _____ formally ended the Thirty Years' War.
    (a) Peace of Prague
    (b) Peace of Augsburg
    (c) Peace of Westphalia
    (d) Edict of Restitution

True-False

_____1. The early sixteenth and mid-seventeenth centuries were commonly referred to as an age of religious wars.

_____2. Among the three families struggling to gain control of the French monarchy after the accidental death of Henry II, the Guises were Catholic reactionaries.

_____3. Both Henry III and Henry IV of France were assassinated as a result of bitter religious feelings in France.

_____4. By the early seventeenth century, Europe's population had reached about 1 million.

_____5. Since both were staunch Catholic leaders, the marriage of Philip of Spain and Mary I of England was popularly supported in both countries.

_____6. The growing English influence on the high seas was demonstrated toward the end of the sixteenth century when Sir Francis Drake circumnavigated the globe.

_____7. An important cause of the Thirty Years' War was the awakening of German nationalism in the early seventeenth century.

_____8. On the eve of the Thirty Years' War, Bavaria and the Palatinate agreed to settle their religious differences.

_____9. The 1629 Edict of Restitution was a dramatic milestone in the reconciliation of Calvinists with Lutherans and Catholics.

_____10. Spain's spectacular victories against France in the period after 1648 led to the Treaty of the Pyrenees.

Completion

1. _____ was the man who ascended the French throne in 1589.

2. The _____ formally sanctioned minority religious rights within predominately Catholic France.

3. The naval battle of _____ temporarily gave Spain control of the Mediterranean.

4. _____ became a Calvinist after the St. Bartholomew's Day Massacre.

5. In 1553, Mary I's right to the English throne was challenged by _____ .

6. The English separatists who wanted absolutely no outside interference with their religious groups were the _____ .

7. _____ was the author of the First Blast of the Trumpet Against the Terrible Regiment of Women.

8. _____ granted the German political entities a degree of sovereignty.

9. The most important center for Calvinism outside of Geneva was the German city of _____ .

10. _____ acquired a significant amount of territory by the end of the Thirty Years' War.

When

1. In what year was Henry IV assassinated?
   - (a) 1589
   - (b) 1598
   - (c) 1600
   - (d) 1610

2. How many Turks died in the naval battle of Lepanto?
   - (a) 10,000
   - (b) 20,000
   - (c) 30,000
   - (d) 35,000

3. When did Queen Elizabeth die?
   - (a) February 18, 1587
   - (b) September 13, 1598
   - (c) May 30, 1588
   - (d) March 23, 1603

4. The French entered the Thirty Years' War in 1635. Because of their entrance, how much longer did the war last?
   - (a) 11 years
   - (b) 12 years
   - (c) 13 years
   - (d) 14 years

5. In what year was Catholism embraced by Henry IV?
   - (a) 1562
   - (b) 1572
   - (c) 1589
   - (d) 1593

Matching

Match the leader to his/her country.

Henry II	Spain
Philip II	Denmark
Mary Tudor	Bohemia
Ferdinand	England
Christian IV	France

Map Labeling

Using Map 12-3, identify (by labeling) 1 to 2 cities that were under rule following:

Swedish dominions   The Spanish Monarchy   Church Lands

Brandenburg Prussia   Austria Habsburg

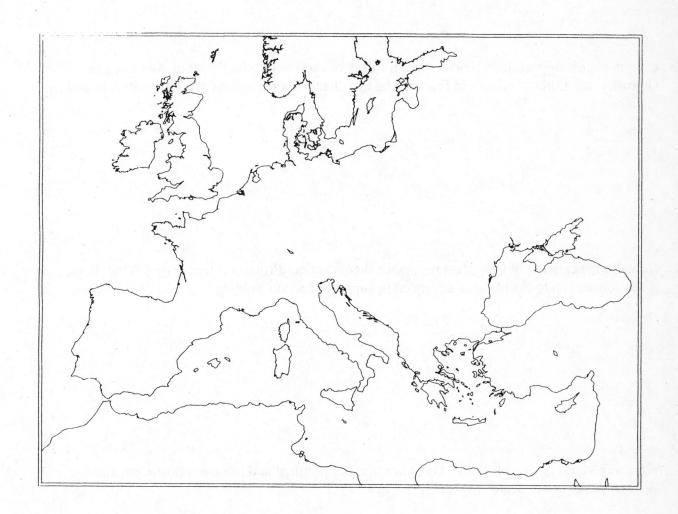

How and Why

1. In reviewing the study of the Reformation what would you describe as the most central teachings of the Catholics, the Lutherans, and the Calvinists?

2. Compare and contrast the religious compromises worked out in the Peace of Augsburg in Germany, the Edict of Nantes in France, and the Elizabethan religious settlement in England.

3. How did the concept of Protestant resistance theory reflect Protestant teachings? What, if any, is the connection to the theories advanced in support of witch-hunting?

4. Who was Mary, Queen of Scots? Trace her life, her political and religious positions, and the circumstances of her death.

5. List in detail the terms of the Treaty of Westphalia. In your opinion, which of these terms appears to have had a lasting effect on the peoples of Europe?

Chapter 13
PATHS TO CONSTITUTIONALISM AND ABSOLUTISM:
ENGLAND AND FRANCE
IN THE SEVENTEENTH CENTURY

Practice Test

1. The book, *A Trew Law of Free Monarchies* was written by
   (a) James VI of Scotland.
   (b) John Locke.
   (c) Charles I.
   (d) Oliver Cromwell.

2. The Clarendon Code excluded which groups from religious and political offices?
   (a) Roman Catholics
   (b) Independents
   (c) Presbyterians
   (d) all of the above

3. The so-called Test Act was largely aimed at discrediting
   (a) Titus Oates.
   (b) James, duke of York.
   (c) Charles II.
   (d) Earl of Shaftsbury.

4. The reason for the continuing opposition to the reign of James II was his
   (a) imprisonment of Anglican bishops.
   (b) appointments of known Catholics to high offices.
   (c) insistence upon the repeal of the Test Act.
   (d) all of the above

5. Which king set the goal, "one king, one law, one faith"?
   (a) George I
   (b) Henry IV
   (c) Louis XIV
   (d) James II

6. _____ was least directly responsible for the establishment of absolutism in France during the seventeenth century.
   (a) Louis XIII
   (b) Sully
   (c) Richelieu
   (d) Mazarin

7. Jansenists believed that
    (a) original sin had been redeemed through Christ's death.
    (b) Cornelis Jansen should be canonized.
    (c) original sin could not be redeemed without special grace from God.
    (d) St. Augustine had incorrectly interpreted the concept of original sin.

8. The marquis of Louvois is noted for
    (a) establishing a professional French army.
    (b) his superior military tactics.
    (c) introducing a merit-based system of promotion within the French army.
    (d) all of the above

9. Louis XIV considered the revocation of the Edict of Nantes
    (a) unimportant.
    (b) militarily significant.
    (c) his most pious act.
    (d) good for business.

10. Sebastien Vaubau was an extremely intelligent military engineer who
    (a) brought defending and invading towns to a new art.
    (b) invented trench warfare.
    (c) developed the concept of defensive frontiers that were used through WW I.
    (d) all of the above

True-False

_____1. John Pym was among the important leaders of Parliament who opposed the policies of Charles I.

_____2. The alliance with Scottish Presbyterians and the reorganization of the army under Parliament assured the Puritan victory over Charles I.

_____3. Charles II of England died a Roman Catholic.

_____4. The English Toleration Act of 1689 granted religious freedom to all but the most radical religious groups.

_____5. Despite his persecution of the Huguenots at home, Cardinal Richelieu allied France with Swedish Protestants during the Thirty Years' War.

_____6. Throughout the seventeenth century, the Catholic Jansenists allied with the Jesuits against French Huguenots.

_____7. Jean-Baptiste Colbert's economic policies had the effect of diminishing France's industrial and commercial potential.

_____8.   In reality, the revocation of the Edict of Nantes came as a complete surprise.

_____9.   Philip of Anjou was the grandson of Louis XIV.

_____10. From a military perspective, regarding each of the wars fought in the reign of Louis XIV, France was best prepared for the War of Spanish Succession.

Completion

1. James VI of Scotland, who became James I of England, was the son of _____ .

2. The religious minister under Charles I was _____ and, in the 1630s, he provoked a war with Scotland.

3. The fate of Charles I appears to have been sealed when Cromwell's New Model Army defeated him at _____ in June 1645.

4. The largest military engagement of the English Civil War was the 1644 battle at _____ .

5. _____ was the official title used by Oliver Cromwell after taking power in 1653.

6. The so-called "Glorious Revolution" in England was justified in the work titled *Second Treatise on Government* written by _____ .

7. A _____ was a labor tax that drafted workers to build and maintain roads.

8. One of the most important factors in establishing absolutism in France was the systematic reduction of the influence of the _____ .

9. The most famous of the defenders of the Jansenist movement was _____ .

10. _____ is the name used to describe the financial policies of the French minister Colbert.

When

1. The King James version of the Bible appeared in
   (a)   1609.
   (b)   1610.
   (c)   1611.
   (d)   1612.

2. What century was referred to as the "century of strife"?
  (a) fourteenth
  (b) fifteenth
  (c) sixteenth
  (d) seventeenth

3. The correct order of these important treaties negotiated during the wars of Louis XIV would be
  (a) Utrecht-Rastadt, Ryswick, Nijmwegen.
  (b) Nijmwegen, Ryswick, Utrecht-Rastadt.
  (c) Ryswick, Nijmwegen, Ais-la-Chapelle.
  (d) Nijmwegen, Utrecht-Rastadt, Ryswick .

4. Jansenism first appeared in the
  (a) 1620s.
  (b) 1630s.
  (c) 1640s.
  (d) 1650s.

5. In what year was the monarch restored to England?
  (a) 1642
  (b) 1649
  (c) 1660
  (d) 1685

Matching

Match the term to its correct definition

Intendants   followed the teachings of St. Augustine

Arminians   oversaw the conduct of the aristocracy in the provinces thorough
                         widespread rebellions that tried to reverse the drift toward absolute
                         monarch and preserving local autonomy

Fronde   a plan to establish absolute monarchy through strict efficiency and
                         administrative centralization

Jansenism   rejected Puritan doctrines and championed elaborate services of worship

Map Labeling

Using the map provided, label the year that Louis invaded the following cities and/or countries.

Flanders   Strasbourg
Amsterdam   Franche-Comte

How and Why

1. English politics during the seventeenth century was a blend of religious concerns and monarchial decline. How does the reign of Elizabeth I in the previous century set the stage for the struggle between king and Parliament in this era?

2. What factors do you consider important in assessing the success of the Puritans during Cromwell's era?

3. Assess the roles of Cardinals Richelieu and Mazarin in the establishment of absolutism in France.

4. Examine the reign of Louis XIV. What were his successes and what were his failures?

5. Compare and contrast the development of the governments of England and France during the seventeenth century. Answer with specific references to persons, statutes, and events as needed.

Chapter 14
NEW DIRECTIONS IN THOUGHT AND CULTURE IN THE SIXTEENTH AND SEVENTEENTH CENTURIES

Practice Test

1. Which of the following expressions best characterizes the nature of the Scientific Revolution?
    (a) It occurred several places in Europe at the same time.
    (b) It was not revolutionary in the normal sense of the word.
    (c) It was a complex movement involving many persons.
    (d) all of the above

2. Whom of the following actually opposed Copernicus's views?
    (a) Tycho Brahe
    (b) Johannes Kepler
    (c) Galileo Galilei
    (d) Francis Bacon

3. Who of the following popularized the Copernican system and articulated the concept of a universe subject to mathematical laws?
    (a) Galileo
    (b) Bacon
    (c) Locke
    (d) Kepler

4. Francis Bacon was NOT a
    (a) lawyer.
    (b) statesman.
    (c) scientist.
    (d) author.

5. The belief that human knowledge should produce useful results was held by
    (a) Francis Bacon.
    (b) Johannes Kepler.
    (c) Descartes.
    (d) none of the above

6. Analytic geometry was first developed by
    (a) Galileo.
    (b) Brahe.
    (c) Descartes.
    (d) none of the above

7. Pascal believed that
    (a)   there was danger in following traditional religious ways.
    (b)   misery loves company.
    (c)   God's mercy was for everyone.
    (d)   it is better to believe in God than not to.

8. The religious thought associated with deducing of religious conclusions from nature became known as
    (a)   econo-theology.
    (b)   naturo-theology.
    (c)   physico-theology.
    (d)   none of the above

9. In Thomas Hobbes's view, man was
    (a)   a person neither good nor evil.
    (b)   a self-centered beast.
    (c)   essentially God-fearing.
    (d)   none of the above

10. Locke believed in all of the following EXCEPT
    (a) government should limit themselves to protecting property.
    (b) government should be responsive to the wishes of the governed.
    (c) government should interfere in the religious lives of its citizens.
    (d) governments mean to protect human liberty, not restrain it.

True-False

_____1.   Nicolaus Copernicus found the Ptolemaic system of the universe to be mathematically clumsy and inconsistent.

_____2.   Tycho Brahe advocated an earth-centered system to astronomy.

_____3.   Galileo popularized the Copernican system and articulated the concept of a universe subject to mathematical laws.

_____4.   The proponents of the new science sought to explain the world in terms of mechanical metaphors, or the language of machinery.

_____5.   Newton believed that mathematics was the key to understanding nature.

_____6.   The Englishman Francis Bacon is considered to be the founder of empiricism and experimentation in science.

_____7.   In 1632, René Descartes wrote Dialogues on the *Two Chief Systems of the World.*

_____8.   Locke believed that knowledge was innate.

_____9.   In the seventeenth century, no one really believed in the power of demons.

_____10. Thomas Hobbes supported the idea of a strong and efficient ruler because he believed such a ruler would alleviate the dangers for humans existing in the state of nature.

Completion

1. The Ptolemaic view of the universe is found in a work written in the second century and titled the _____ .

2. The work of _____ expanded on the previous efforts of Nicolaus Copernicus and Tycho Brahe.

3. For Galileo, the rationality for the entire universe was based on _____ .

4. The work of _____ focused on the issue of planetary motion and established a basis for physics.

5. _____ invented analytic geometry.

6. In the *Leviathan*, _____ portrayed human beings and society in a thoroughly materialistic and mechanical way.

7. _____ encouraged individuals to challenge tradition and look toward change and innovation.

8. The political philosopher Thomas Hobbes believed that the dangers of _____ were greater than the dangers of tyranny.

9   _____ was the author of *Grounds of Natural Philosophy*.

10. _____ believed that human beings were capable of goodwill and rational behavior.

When

1. Which of the following works was written first?
    (a) *On the Revolutions of Heavenly Spheres*
    (b) *The New Astronomy*
    (c) *Leviathan*
    (d) *Ethics*

2. In what year was the Copernican theory condemned by the Catholic Church?
  (a) 1630
  (b) 1631
  (c) 1632
  (d) 1633

3. Witch trials cam to an end in the
  (a) late sixteenth century.
  (b) early seventeenth century.
  (c) mid-seventeenth century.
  (d) late seventeenth century.

4. Astronomy was first studied through a telescope in
  (a) 1509.
  (b) 1510.
  (c) 1609.
  (d) 1610.

5. In what year was Galileo's text *Dialogue on the Two Chief World Systems* published?
  (a) 1616
  (b) 1623
  (c) 1632
  (d) none of the above

Matching

Match the author to his work.

Kepler	*Treaties of Government*
Locke	*Principia Mathematica*
Bacon	*The New Astronomy*
Galileo	*Novum Organum*
Newton	*The Starry Messenger*

How and Why

1. Describe the roles of Nicolaus Copernicus and Francis Bacon in influencing what is now referred to as the Scientific Revolution.

2. Give a brief description of how the new science challenged the old way of understanding religion. Pinpoint two major fronts.

3. Discuss the central characteristics of the thought of Thomas Hobbes. Are there parts of his work that are reflected in modern times?

4. Contrast Hobbes's view of authority with that of John Locke. Why is Locke considered so influential even in modern times?

Chapter 15
SUCCESSFUL AND UNSUCCESSFUL PATHS TO POWER (1686–1740)

Practice Test

1. According to the text, which of the following countries was NOT moving forward in this period?
   (a) Great Britain
   (b) Russia
   (c) Spain
   (d) Prussia

2. Which of the following contributed LEAST to the decline of the Netherlands in the eighteenth century?
   (a) the fishing industry
   (b) shipbuilding
   (c) the financial community
   (d) various domestic industries

3. The Mississippi Company
   (a) was the brainchild of John Law.
   (b) was responsible for the management of the French national debt.
   (c) ended the financial career of John Law.
   (d) all of the above

4. During the eighteenth century, the English Parliament was dominated by
   (a) the old aristocracy.
   (b) the rising middle class.
   (c) owners of property.
   (d) representatives of the people.

5. As one moved farther eastward in Europe in the eighteenth century, there was increasing likelihood of finding
   (a) rotten boroughs.
   (b) serfdom.
   (c) prominent intellectuals.
   (d) larger navies.

6. During this period of time, Sweden's weakness was in her
   (a) economy.
   (b) army.
   (c) location on the Baltic Sea.
   (d) none of the above.

7. In the early eighteenth century a major defeat of Sweden occurred in the battle of
   - (a) Poltava.
   - (b) Regensburg.
   - (c) Narva.
   - (d) none of the above

8. Beginning in this era, a major factor in European international relations was the decline of
   - (a) the Ottoman Empire.
   - (b) Poland.
   - (c) Russia.
   - (d) Austria.

9. The General-Ober-Finanz-Kriegs-und-Domänen-Direktorium is normally associated with the state of
   - (a) Russia.
   - (b) Poland.
   - (c) Prussia.
   - (d) the Holy Roman Empire.

10. When Russia entered into the political arena, many viewed it as
   - (a) a formidable force in Europe.
   - (b) a country with warm-water ports.
   - (c) a vast land with unexploited potential.
   - (d) none of the above

True-False

_____1. The Netherlands didn't experience much internal strife because it tolerated different religions.

_____2. The chief feature of French political life in the eighteenth century until the French Revolution (1789) was the attempt of the nobility to limit monarchial power.

_____3. Louis XV of France is considered a failure not only because of his mediocrity, but because he was never properly trained as a ruler, was lazy, and given to vice.

_____4. Both Whigs and Tories were proponents of the status quo in England, yet the Tories supported urban commercial interests and were in favor of religious toleration in general.

_____5. Control of the House of Commons could be achieved by the careful use of patronage and electoral management of the boroughs in England.

_____6. By the end of the seventeenth century, warfare and the resultant shifting political alliances had become basic ingredients of life in central Europe.

_____7.   The Pragmatic Sanction was designed to ensure the succession to the Austrian throne of Maria Theresa.

_____8.   The Hohenzollern rulers of Prussia received the title of King, in recognition of the marriage of Frederick William I to Maria Theresa.

_____9.   As a result of frequent revolutions, military conspiracies, and assassinations the Romanovs ruled Russia for only 100 years.

_____10.   Peter's son, Aleksei, conspired against his father during the Great Northern War.

Completion

1. The Netherlands emerged as a nation after revolting against _____ in 1572.

2. Though not having the power to legislate, the _____ of France became effective centers of resistance to royal authority.

3. The most influential minister in the reign of France's Louis XV was the aged _____ .

4. In reality _____ could be considered the first Prime Minister of Great Britain.

5. By laying siege to the city of _____ in 1683, the Turks were able to demonstrate the power of the Ottoman Empire.

6. The liberiim veto was a practice exercised in the central legislative assembly of _____ .

7. The rise of the Hohenzollern family to control of Prussia began with their rule of the German territory of _____ .

8. _____ were the important class of German nobility influential throughout Prussian history.

9. In 1722, Peter the Great attempted to rearrange the Russian nobility through the _____ .

10. An early attempt at religious reform in Russia was led by the Patriarch _____ .

When

1. In what year was France more of a power to reckon with?
   - (a) 1715
   - (b) 1680
   - (c) 1690
   - (d) 1700

2. During what century was Poland purported to disappear from the map of Europe?
   - (a) the seventeenth
   - (b) the late seventeenth
   - (c) the eighteenth
   - (d) the late eighteenth

3. Which of the following occurred first?
   - (a) Russia defeated in the battle at Narva
   - (b) European tour of Peter the Great
   - (c) Saint Petersburg founded
   - (d) end of the Great Northern War

4. When did the Great Northern War begin?
   - (a) 1699
   - (b) 1700
   - (c) 1799
   - (d) 1800

5. What is the correct order of events?
   - (a) St. Petersburg founded; Walpole dominates British politics; Michael Romanov becomes tsar; Turkish siege of Vienna
   - (b) Michael Romanov becomes tsar; Walpole dominates British politics; St. Petersburg founded; Turkish siege of Vienna
   - (c) Michael Romanov becomes tsar; Turkish siege of Vienna; St. Petersburg founded; Walpole dominates British politics
   - (d) Turkish siege of Vienna; St. Petersburg founded; Michael Romanov becomes tsar; Walpole dominates British politics

Matching

Match the party to what it supported.

Tories   received public offices and patronage, wanted to see peace with France, stressed religious toleration for Protestant nonconformists

Whigs   favored a strong monarch, defended commerical interests firmly supported the Anglican Church

Map Labeling

Identify the five areas that the Habsburgs consolidated their power over from 1521-1772. Place an asterisk next to those areas on the map. (Map 15-2)

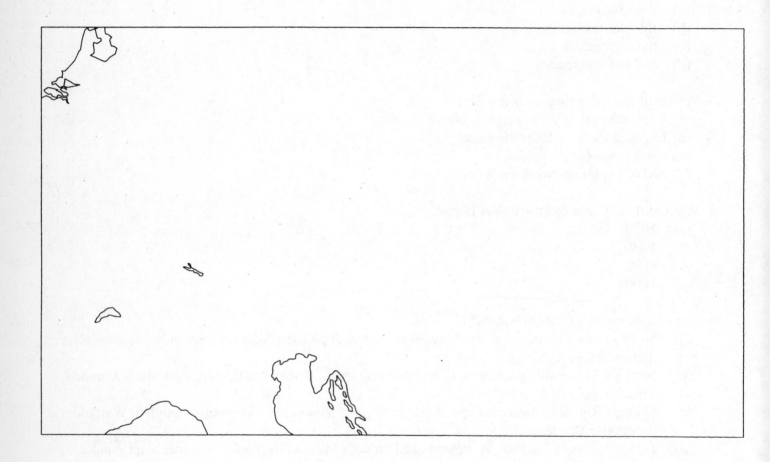

How and Why

1. Describe the development of parliamentary government in England in the first half of the eighteenth century. What kind of compromises made this unique system work?

2. How does the development of central authority in Prussia differ from that in other European states during this period? How was it similar?

3. Why were the so-called "reform" efforts of Russia's Peter the Great successful only in part?

4. Generally characterize the differences between the Eastern European states [Sweden, Poland, Austria, Prussia, and Russia] and the Western states [France and England].

5. In a review of the states of eighteenth-century Europe, which one(s) would you consider as showing the most promise for the future, and why?

LECTURE COMPANION

The following lecture note pages can be used to record your instructor's lectures and assignments for each chapter.

Chapter 1
THE BIRTH OF CIVILIZATION

Lecture Notes   Date:_____

Chapter 2
THE RISE OF GREEK CIVILIZATION

Lecture Notes   **Date:**_____

Chapter 3
CLASSICAL AND HELLENISTIC GREECE

Lecture Notes   **Date:**_____

Chapter 4
ROME: FROM REPUBLIC TO EMPIRE

Lecture Notes   **Date:**_____

Chapter 5
THE ROMAN EMPIRE

Lecture Notes   Date:_____

Chapter 6
THE EARLY MIDDLE AGES (476-1000): THE BIRTH OF EUROPE

Lecture Notes   Date:_____

Chapter 7
THE HIGH MIDDLE AGES (1000–1300):
THE ASCENDENCY OF THE CHURCH AND THE RISE OF STATES

Lecture Notes   **Date:**_____

Chapter 8
THE HIGH MIDDLE AGES (100–1300): PEOPLE, TOWNS, AND UNIVERSITIES

Lecture Notes   **Date:**_____

Chapter 9
THE LATE MIDDLE AGES (1300–1527):
CENTURIES OF CRISIS

Lecture Notes   **Date:**_____

Chapter 10
RENAISSANCE AND DISCOVERY

Lecture Notes   **Date:**_____

Chapter 11
THE AGE OF REFORMATION

Lecture Notes   **Date:**_____

Chapter 12
THE AGE OF RELIGIOUS WARS

Lecture Notes   **Date:**_____

Chapter 13
PATHS TO CONSTITUTIONALISM AND ABSOLUTISM: ENGLAND AND FRANCE IN THE SEVENTEENTH CENTURY

Lecture Notes   **Date:**_____

Chapter 14
NEW DIRECTIONS IN THOUGHT AND CULTURE IN THE SIXTEENTH AND SEVENTEENTH CENTURIES

Lecture Notes   **Date:**_____

Chapter 15
SUCCESSFUL AND UNSUCCESSFUL PATHS TO POWER
(1686–1740)

Lecture Notes   **Date:**_____

ANSWER KEY

Chapter 1
Practice Test
1.B
2.A
3.D
4.C
5.B
6.D
7.C
8.B
9.A
10.D

True/False
1.T
2.F
3.T
4.F
5.F
6.F
7.F
8.F
9.F
10.F

Completion
1.Neolithic
2. Sumerians
3.Sargon
4.Gilgamesh
5.Amunhotep IV
6.Palestine
7.Phoenicians
8.monotheism
9.Sekhmet
10.Thales

When
1. A
2. C
3. B
4. C
5. B

Matching
Paleolithic—old stone
Bronze Age—increasing importance on metal
Cuneiform—very first writing system
Neolithic—new stone "age"
Pharaoh—god-king of ancient Egypt
Monotheism—belief in one God

Map Labeling
Civilization's first appearance—Babylon
Earliest urban center—Uruk
First monarachs—Kish
Final flowering of Sumerian civilization—Ur
New Amorite dynasties—Isin Larsa

Chapter 2
Practice Test
1.C
2.C
3.C
4.D
5.A
6.C
7.A
8.B
9.C
10.D

True-False
1.F
2.T
3.F
4.F
5.T
6.T
7.F
8.F
9.T
10.F

Completion
1. palaces
2. Linear B
3. Homer
4. hoplite phalanx
5. tyrants
6. Delphi
7. Dionysus
8. noble/base
9. Sparta
10. Attica/Salamis

When
1. B
2. B
3. C
4. B
5. B

Matching
Zeus—a sky god
Demeter—goddess of agriculture and marriage
Hera—Zeus's wife and sister

Ares—god of strife
Hermes—cunning messenger god

Map Labeling
Two major cites—Sparta and Athens
Magna Graecia—the area between Italy and Sicily
Island leveled—Naxos
Greeks on the Western Coast—Ionians

Chapter 3
Practice Test
1.B
2.C
3.C
4.C
5.D
6.D
7.A
8.D
9.C
10.D

True/False
1.T
2.T
3.F
4.F
5.T
6.F
7.F
8.F
9.T
10.F

Completion
1. Cimon
2. Sparta/Athens
3. Thales
4. Thucydides
5. Diogenes/Cynics
6. phalanx
7. Isocrates
8. Skeptics
9. death
10. Logos

When
1. C
2. B
3. B
4. D
5. A

Matching

Thales   all things come from a single universal element: water
Heraclitus   permanence is an illusion
Sophists   the art of persuasion through rhetoric
Socrates   truth and the power of reason
Empedocles   world is composed of permanent elements
Aristotle   the world is constantly evolving from potentiality to actuality

Map Labeling
Independent Members: Pagasae, Thebes, Athens, Argos
Dependent Members: Sparta, Olympia, Epidaurus

Chapter 4
Practice Test
1. C
2. B
3. D
4. D
5. D
6. C
7. A
8. D
9. C
10. D

True-False
1. F
2. T
3. F
4. T
5. T
6. T
7. F
8. F
9. T
10. T

Completion
1. family
2. Pyrrhic victory
3. Hannibal Barca
4. paedagogous
5. latifundia
6. C. Marius
7. Spartacus
8. G. Julius Caesar
9. Octavian
10. Gaius Cassius Longinus/Marcus Junius Brutus

When

1. B
2. C
3. D
4. D
5. A

Matching
Publius Cornelius Scipio—Battle of Zama
C. Marins—Jugurthine War
Pompey—slave rebellion led by Spartacus
Caesar—Gaul
Octavio—Actium

Map Labeling
Three provinces of the Roman Empire: Sicily, Sardinia, Corsica
City Hamilcar Bara restored: Carthage
Romans violated the Ebro Treaty and allied themselves with: Saguntum
Port where Romans faced disaster: Syracuse

Chapter 5
Practice Test
1. D
2. C
3. D
4. B
5. D
6. C
7. D
8. C
9. B
10. B

True-False
1. F
2. F
3. F
4. T
5. T
6. F
7. T
8. T
9. T
10. F

Completion
1. Greek or Hellenistic
2. Vergil
3. Vespasian
4. Silver Age
5. Messiah
6. agape or love feast, Eucharist or thanksgiving
7. Byzantine
8. Decius

9. Trinity
10. Christianity

When
1. D
2. B
3. C
4. C
5. A

Matching
Cicero	Treaties on rhetoric, ethics, politics
Lucretius	*De Rerum Natura*
Horace	*Satires*
Propertius	Elegies
Ovid	Metamorphoses

Map Labeling
1. Dacia
2. Parthian Empire
3. Armenia, Assyria, Mesopotamia
4. Wall of Hadrian

Chapter 6
Practice Test
1. A
2. D
3. A
4. B
5. C
6. D
7. D
8. A
9. C
10. A

True-False
1. T
2. F
3. T
4. F
5. T
6. F
7. F
8. T
9. F
10. F

Completion
1. Theodora
2. Mecca
3. Hegira
4. Averroes
5. Anthony of Egypt
6. papal primacy

7.King Clovis
8.Poitiers
9.Alcuin
10.benefice/fief

7. Hastings
8. Domesday Book
9. Philip Augustus
10. Pope Innocent

When
1. C
2. D
3. B
4. D
5. C

When
1. C
2. B
3. C
4. B
5. B

Matching
Code—revised imperial edits
Novellae—Justinian's decrees
Digest—summarized opinions of famous legal experts
Institutes—textbook for training authors

Matching
Innocent—2 new sects
Henry II—creation of the English-French Empire
Louis IX—embodiment of the perfect ruler
Frederick II—ended Otto IVs treacherous reign
Pope Gregory IX—canonization of Francis of Assisi

Map Labeling
1. Papal States
2. Corsica
3. Aachen

Map Labeling
1. Sicily
2. Mainz
3. Aachen
4. Sicily
5. Lombardy

Chapter 7
Practice Test
1.D
2.A
3.D
4.B
5.B
6.A
7.D
8.C
9.B
10.C

Chapter 8
Practice Test
1.C
2.C
3.B
4.B
5.C
6.D
7.D
8.C
9.B
10.D

True-False
1.T
2.T
3.F
4.T
5.T
6.T
7.F
8.F
9.T
10.F

True-False
1.T
2.T
3.F
4.T
6.T
7.F
8.F
9.F
5.T
10. F

Completion
1. Henry I, the Fowler
2. Pope Stephen IX
3. Concordat at Worms
4. Urban II
5. The Fourth Lateran Council
6. Thomas Aquinas

Completion
1. knighthood
2. nobility
3. banalities

4. guilds
5. towns/kings
6. Bologna
7. mobility
8. Paris
9. Four Books of Sentences
10. inherity, administer, dispose of, bequeath

When
1. C
2. C
3. D
4. B
5. C

Matching
Knights—protection
Clergy—prayer intervention
Peasants—land workers
Village artisans—production of supplies
Secular clergy—work among the laity

Map Labeling
1. Damascus
2. Moscow, Novgorod
3. Naples
4. Toledo; Cordoba
5. Kiev

Chapter 9
Practice Test
1. C
2. D
3. D
4. B
5. A
6. A
7. A
8. D
9. B
10. C

True-False
1. F
2. T
3. T
4. T
5. F
6. T
7. T
8. T
9. F
10. T

Completion
1. longbow

2. Jacquerie
3. nationalism
4. Decameron
5. Church/state
6. William of Ockham
7. University of Prague
8. John Huss
9. Execrabilis
10. the Great Russians, the White Russians, the little Russians or Ukrainians

When
1. D
2. B
3. B
4. D
5. A

Map Labeling
1. Calais
2. Near Poitiers
3. Normandy
4. Orleans
5. Calais

Matching
Gregory XI—agreed to move the papacy from Avignon to Rome
Clement VI—sold indulgences
Clement V—increased papal taxation of the clergy
John XXII—excommunicated William of Ockham
Benedict XII—began construction of a palace at Avignon

Chapter 10
Practice Test
1. D
2. B
3. B
4. A
5. C
6. D
7. D
8. A
9. B
10. B

True-False
1. F
2. F
3. T
4. F
5. F
6. F

7.F
8.T
9.F
10.T

Completion
1.   Venice
2.   Dante Alighieri/Francesco Petrarch
3.   The Book of the Courtier
4.   Lorenzo Valla
5.   The School of Athens
6.   Estates General
7.   Castile/Aragon
8.   Desiderius Erasmus
9.   Johann Reuchlin
10. capitalism

When
1. B
2. B
3. C
4. D
5. C

Matching
Petrarch—*Letters to the Ancient Dead*
Dante Alighieri—*Divine Comedy*
Boccaccio—*Decameron*
Christine de Pisan—*The City of Ladies*
Quintilian—*Education of the Orator*

Map Labeling
1. Guinea
2. Canary Islands
3. 1519

Chapter 11
Practice Test
1.D
2.B
3.C
4.C
5.D
6.B
7.A
8.D
9.D
10.C

True-False
1.T
2.T
3.F
4.T
5. F
6.T

7.F
8.T
9.T
10.F

Completion
1.   Modern Devotion, or Brothers of the Common Life
2.   Imitation of Christ
3.   Wittenberg
4.   Ulrich Zwingli
5.   Conrad Grebel
6.   Cardinal Wolsey
7.   Act of Supremacy
8.   Trent
9.   laity, or ordinary persons
10. women

When
1. B
2. A
3.A
4. D
5. D

Matching
Anne Boleyn—charged with treason and adultery and was beheaded
Jane Seymour—gave Henry a male heir—Edward
Anne of Cleves—forged an alliance among Protestant princes
Catherine Howard—beheaded for adultery
Catherine Parr—a patron of humanists and reforms—outlived Henry

Map Labeling
Wittenberg
n/a
Geneva
Bavaria
Rome

Chapter 12
Practice Test
1.A
2.D
3.A
4.C
5.B
6.C
7.C
8.B
9.B
10.C

True-False
1. F
2. T
3. T
4. F
5. F
6. T
7. F
8. F
9. F
10. F

Completion
1. Henry of Navarre or Henry IV
2. Edict of Nantes
3. Lepanto
4. William of Orange
5. Lady Jane Grey
6. Congregationalists
7. John Knox
8. Peace of Augsburg
9. Heidelberg
10. France

When
1. D
2. C
3. D
4. C
5. D

Matching
Henry II—France
Philip II—Spain
Mary Tudor—England
Ferdinand—Bohemia
Christian IV—Denmark

Map Labeling
Answers will vary—some are given here
Swedish—Stockholm
Austria—Vienna, Prague
Church Lands—Rome, Bologna

Chapter 13
Practice Test
1. A
2. D
3. B
4. D
5. c
6. A
7. C
8. D
9. C
10. d

True-False
1. T
2. T
3. T
4. F
5. T
6. F
7. F
8. T
9. T
10. F

Completion
1. Mary Stuart, Queen of Scots
2. William Laud
3. Naseby
4. Marston Moor
5. Lord Protector
6. John Locke
7. corvee
8. parlements
9. Blaise Pascal
10. Mercantilism

When
1. C
2. D
3. B
4. B
5. C

Matching
Intendants-- oversaw the conduct of the aristocracy in the provinces
Arminians— rejected Puritan doctrines and championed elaborate services of worship
Thorough— a plan to establish absolute monarchy through strict efficiency and administrative centralization
Fronde— widespread rebellions that tried to reverse the drift toward absolute monarchy and preserving local autonomy
Jansenism—followed the teachings of St. Augustine

Map Labeling

Flanders—1667
Amsterdam—1672
Strasbourg—1681
Franche-Comte—1667

Chapter 14
Practice Test
1. D

2.A
3.A
4. C
5.A
6.C
7.D
8.C
9.B
10.C

True-False
1.T
2.T
3.T
4.T
5. T
6.T
7.F
8.F
9.F
10.T

Completion
1. Almagest
2. Johannes Kepler
3. mathematics
4. Isaac Newton
5. René Descartes
6. Thomas Hobbes
7. Francis Bacon
8. anarchy
9. Margaret Cavendish
10. John Locke

When
1. A
2. D
3. D
4. C
5. C

Matching
Kepler—*The New Astronomy*
Locke—*Treatises of Government*
Bacon—*Movum Organum*
Galileo—*The Starry Messenger*
Newton—*Principia Mathematica*

Chapter 15
Practice Test
1.C
2.C
3.D
4.C
5.B
6.A

7.A
8.A
9.C
10.C

True-False
1.T
2.T
3.T
4.F
5.T
6.T
7.T
8.F
9.F
10.T

Completion
1. Spain
2. parliaments
3. Cardinal Fleury
4. Robert Walpole
5. Vienna
6. Poland
7. Brandenburg
8. Junkers
9. Table of Ranks
10. Nikon

When
1. B
2. C
3. B
4. B
5. C

Matching
Tories—wanted to see peace with France; favored a strong monarch; firmly supported the Anglican Church
Whigs—received public offices and patronage; stressed religious toleration for Protestant nonconformists; defended commercial interests

Map Labeling
Transylvania
Hungary
Croatia
Bohemia
Austria